THE PEOPLE'S BIBLE

"The King James Bible moulded thinking and writing in English for 400 years. Derek Wilson's book – divinely well-informed, devilishly entertaining – helps us understand how one of the world's most influential texts took shape, and tells the story of its once strong and now faltering grip on English-speaking imaginations."

Felipe Fernandez-Armesto, William P. Reynolds
Professor of History, University of Notre Dame

The People's Bible

The Remarkable History of the King James Version

Derek Wilson

LION

Copyright © 2010 Derek Wilson
This edition copyright © 2010 Lion Hudson

The author asserts the moral right
to be identified as the author of this work

A Lion Book
an imprint of
Lion Hudson plc
Wilkinson House, Jordan Hill Road,
Oxford OX2 8DR, England
www.lionhudson.com
ISBN 978 0 7459 5351 9

Distributed by:
UK: Marston Book Services, PO Box 269, Abingdon, Oxon, OX14 4YN
USA: Trafalgar Square Publishing, 814 N. Franklin Street, Chicago, IL 60610
USA Christian Market: Kregel Publications, PO Box 2607, Grand Rapids, MI 49501

First edition 2010
10 9 8 7 6 5 4 3 2 1 0

Acknowledgments

pp. 97, 112, 113, 115, 161–62, 173, 175, 176, 188, 190, 202: Extracts from the
Authorized Version of the Bible (The King James Bible), the rights in which are vested
in the Crown, are reproduced by permission of the Crown's Patentee, Cambridge
University Press. p. 173: Scripture quotation from the *Revised Standard Version* published
by HarperCollins Publishers, copyright © 1989 by the Division of Christian Education
of the National Council of the Churches of Christ in the USA, and are used by
permission. All rights reserved. pp. 175–76: Scripture quotation from *The Jerusalem
Bible* © 1966 by Darton, Longman & Todd Ltd and Doubleday & Company, Inc.

p. 192: Extract taken from *Collected Poems* by Dylan Thomas, published by D Jones,
London 1978. Copyright © David Higham Associates. Used with permission of David
Higham Associates, London. Also, from *The Poems of Dylan Thomas*, copyright © 1952
by Dylan Thomas. Reprinted by permission of New Directions Publishing Corp.

p. 169: Extract taken from *Non-Bourgeois Theology* by J G Donders, published by Orbis
Books 1979. Copyright © J G Donders 1979. Used with permission of Orbis Books,
Maryknoll, USA.

Plate section: Alamy: p. i The Art Gallery Collection; pp. iii, vi (tr) Lebrecht Music and
Arts Photo Library; p. vi (b) The Print Collector; p. vii (b) Michael Jenner; Getty:
p. vi (tl) Verner Reed//Time Life Pictures; Kindra Clineff: p. vii (t); The Bridgeman
Art Library: p. ii (b) Agnew's, London, UK; p. iv–v Claeissens, Anthuenis (Antoon)
(1536–1613)/Private Collection; The National Portrait Gallery, London: p. ii (t); p. viii
illustration from *The Freethinker*, 5 March 1882.

A catalogue record for this book is available from the British Library.

Typeset in 10.5/14 Baskerville Regular
Printed and bound in Great Britain by MPG Books

CONTENTS

FOREWORD

For a nation so wedded to a self-image of tolerance, England has some remarkable skeletons in its cupboard. It was the first kingdom in Europe to expel its entire Jewish population, in 1290. Little more than a century after that, as Derek Wilson points out, it became the only European kingdom to ban the translation of the Bible into the vernacular (at least until the medieval western Latin church got round to an English translation, which somehow it never did). Nevertheless, the English did eventually manage to reverse both these acts of intolerance, and in the second instance, they provided the world with one of its most influential cultural symbols in any language, thanks to the tangled politics of the reign of King James VI of Scotland and I of England and Ireland. The first monarch to unite all the islands of this archipelago under a single crown, James has proved to date perhaps the cleverest occupant of the thrones in these three kingdoms, and he was certainly the most prolific writer to rule in them. So it is fitting that one of his most lasting memorials is a book, albeit one in which he had no personal hand apart from the command that it should be written, consistent encouragement to complete it, and the satisfaction of receiving some unusually extravagant praise from the translators in their preface. And within little more than half a century, this Bible had displaced all its earlier competitors in English. Conservative English-speaking Christians still feel that it has never been surpassed by later efforts to create something more accurately reflecting the original Hebrew and Greek texts. Such Christians, particularly in the United States of America, usually know it by its nickname, "the King James Bible", rather than its official description as the "Authorized Version". It is perhaps ironical that a Bible commissioned by a cheerfully bisexual monarch should still be the standard translation referred to by anglophone Christian fundamentalists in the world's most powerful republic, but history is prone to playing strange tricks.

Derek Wilson guides us from the beginning to the present day, telling first the story of the new vernacular version of the Bible in a language that modern English-speakers might just understand, created by the admirers of John Wycliffe in the late fourteenth century, and then on into the sixteenth-century Reformation which reversed the prohibition on such translations. William Tyndale, an Oxford-trained priest, took up the task anew. His work made him a rebel against the church into which he had been ordained, and led him far from his native Gloucestershire and the medieval religion. New research by Magnus Williamson places him at the beginning of the 1520s, serving in a thoroughly traditional fashion as a chantry priest in Boston parish church before the exile in Germany, which was the setting for his greatest achievement. He paid for translating the Bible into an English now transformed from Wycliffe's time with his imprisonment and death, and his work had to be completed by others. Nevertheless, this strenuous decade of translation in the 1520s and 1530s created the text which King James's translators, now respected clergymen safely ensconced in a Protestant established church, made into something more suited to formal public worship than the urgent vernacular of Tyndale eighty years before. Derek Wilson leads us further, explaining how this great cultural monument of seventeenth-century England took shape, and how its majestic official prose has sustained Christians across the world in very different circumstances over four centuries. The reader should enjoy the zest with which he tells the tale.

Diarmaid MacCulloch
St Cross College, Oxford
Holy Week 2010

CHAPTER 1

IN THE BEGINNING
THERE WAS NO WORD

Christianity has existed in England for over sixteen hundred years and for well over twelve hundred of those years there was no officially approved Bible that the English people could read in their own language. It was not considered necessary that they should do so. The Fourth Lateran Council of the western church decreed in 1215:

> *The secret mysteries of the faith ought not to be explained to all men in all places... For such is the depth of divine Scripture that, not only the simple and illiterate, but even the prudent and learned are not fully sufficient to try to understand it.*

Two centuries later the leaders of the English church went even further by making it a criminal offence to translate any passage of Scripture into the vernacular. Anyone found guilty of doing so faced the prospect of being burned to death as a heretic. England became the only major European country in which translation of the Bible was actually banned.

If we went into a church today, we would probably expect to see a large Bible somewhere or, at least, a lectern from which the Bible is read, so we need to adjust our thinking if we are to comprehend the spiritual, intellectual, and social issues involved in creating what became the most influential book in world history, the King James Version of the Holy Bible. It changed the way people understood their faith and gave expression to their faith. It changed the way they lived their lives and the way they faced death. The story of "how we got our Bible" is the story of a revolution, arguably the most cataclysmic revolution in English history. That is why we need to go back to the beginning, a couple of hundred years before 1604, the year in which the decision was taken to create a royally approved new translation of holy writ.

Just like the people of any other age, the men and women of late medieval England had spiritual needs. The church tried to meet them in various ways. Sermons were preached, although not every Sunday. Few parish clergy had the necessary education to provide regular teaching of any depth. Thus, when a travelling friar from one of the preaching orders – Dominicans, Franciscans, and Augustinians – appeared in the village it was an exciting event. English communities were self-contained and people rarely travelled far from home, so the arrival of a stranger always aroused interest. News would spread quickly that a brown-robed Franciscan or black-robed Dominican had arrived and was to preach in the church or at the market cross, and people would flock to hear him. And what did they hear? Since very few sermons ever got written down and passed on we cannot know. However, what we do have are a few anthologies of sermon illustrations which were provided to help clergy and itinerant preachers to get their message across. For the most part they consist of dramatic or lurid moral tales such as this:

It befell at Dijon, about the year 1240, that a certain usurer would have celebrated his wedding with much rejoicing; and, having been led with instruments of music to the parish church of the Blessed Virgin, and standing now under the church portal that his bride might give her consent and the marriage be ratified according to custom by the promise "I do", and so the wedding might be solemnized in the church by the singing of mass and other ceremonies – while this was there being done, I say, and the bride and bridegroom should have been led with joy into the church, a certain usurer, carved in stone upon the portal above, whom a carven devil was bearing to hell, fell with his money-bag upon the head of this living usurer who should have been married, and crushed and slew him; so that the wedding was turned to mourning, and their joy to lamentation, and the living man was shut out by the stone image from that entrance into church, and those sacraments, from which the priests not only did not exclude him but would have led him in.[1]

Teaching by Images

There was very little else in the way of verbal religious communication in English available to people. The vast majority were illiterate. What handwritten books there were were expensive and in Latin. Church services were also in Latin. So, if the preacher was a reasonably good orator, the impact of his cautionary tales must have been considerable. They help us by giving us some idea of what our medieval ancestors believed and what they understood of the Christian faith.

Thirteenth-century folk lived in a hard world. They were constantly prey to natural calamities, untreatable diseases, and sudden death. Life expectancy was little more than forty-five and at least half of the children who were successfully born died in infancy. People did not doubt that God was active in his world nor that good or ill fortune were signs of his blessing or disapproval. To be sure of divine favour in this world and, more importantly, in the next, they had to avail themselves of whatever aids the church had to offer. After the friar had filled his collecting bag and moved on, his hearers were left with whatever was on offer in the parish church. Here, their eyes were assailed with a profusion of visual images. And it was images, rather than words, which, on a regular basis, fired their imagination and provided them with conduits between earth and heaven.

Every holy building was profusely decorated with the symbols of the faith and stuffed with crucifixes and painted saints. Wherever there was a large surface area of wall or window which could be used, biblical and hagiographical stories were colourfully told. Sculpted and painted images have often been called "sermons in stone" and "the people's Bible". But we have to ask ourselves whether the medieval mind was really capable of grasping the spiritual significance of a carved image and correctly piecing together the story told in a stained glass strip cartoon? The modern visitor needs to study the magnificent west front of Wells Cathedral with the aid of a guide book and can only with difficulty identify the figures in the beautiful windows of King's College Chapel, Cambridge. Were his or her ancestors of 500 years ago better equipped to piece together the main events of the God narrative?

Biblical scenes were comparatively rare in church decoration. Events in the lives of Jesus and the Virgin Mary (many of the latter apocryphal) were featured in some churches, as were some of the more striking Old Testament stories – the creation, Noah's ark, Jonah and the great fish, Abraham offering Isaac, etc. But they had little prominence, being featured, more often than not, in small areas of wood carving. Carver and sculptor rarely applied their chisels with any sense of didactic purpose. They repeated well-known subjects in no particular order and happily mixed sacred and secular motifs. A sequence of roof spandrels in the north aisle of St Mary's Church in Mildenhall, Suffolk, for example, portrays the sacrifice of Isaac, the baptism of Jesus, St George slaying the dragon, and a hunting scene.

Emphasis was more likely to be placed on motifs which supported the ritual life of the church. One popular theme was the seven sacraments. They were usually to be found carved on fonts and on the elaborate font covers, which were among the most remarkable achievements of Gothic craftsmen. The scenes depicted were baptism, confirmation, mass, penance, extreme unction, ordination, and matrimony. Other common features were parades of the Seven Deadly Sins, symbolical and mythological beasts, such as unicorns, griffins, pelicans in their piety, etc. – the list becomes tediously long and we have only considered decoration of a specifically religious character. Mixed up with all these motifs were heraldic devices, and carved scenes inspired by everyday events, as well as flowers, birds, and stylized ornaments of a purely decorative nature. If we are to think of the medieval parish church as a book in which the devout might seek instruction, we should envisage a volume made up of pages torn recklessly from a variety of other books and sewn together in no particular order.

Not only did the conglomeration of vivid images which confronted the worshipper every time he or she went to mass provide scant guidance towards an understanding of the essential elements of the faith, it often distorted truth and created new myths. A typical example is the translation of St Nicholas into the patron saint of children. The most striking feature of Nicholas's life was the large number of converts he made in Asia Minor. Early paintings therefore portrayed him standing beside a font in which stood three naked pagans. In accordance with current artistic convention Nicholas, as the most important figure in the group, was painted as the largest. In later centuries it was assumed that the three diminutive figures were children, and the round barrel-like font was mistaken for a pickling-tub. It remained only for popular piety to weave a legend around the symbols, as follows: One day St Nicholas stayed at an inn not knowing that his host and hostess were murderers. It was their custom to kill and dismember small children, pickle the "joints", and serve them to their guests. The saint was, however, apprised of the situation in a vision. Instead of eating the dainty morsels set before him, he restored them to life.

Thus, the medieval laymen – and most medieval clergy – could make no distinction between biblical and non-biblical events, truth and myth, miracle, and superstition, matters essential to salvation and snares for the credulous.

Holy Materialism

Popular devotion was stirred by stories and images. And material objects. People believed that *things* and *places* could be invested with holiness. Particularly efficacious were the shrines and relics of departed saints. No one doubted that miraculous powers were vested in the bodies, clothes, possessions, and tombs of men and women who had lived holy lives. Christian pilgrimage was the Middle Ages' equivalent of the modern package-tour industry. Churches, abbeys, and cathedrals vied with each other for possession of the most highly celebrated relics, knowing that the penitent, the mendicant, the suffering, and the bereaved would flock to their doors bringing financial proof of their devotion, clamouring to buy candles and souvenirs, and boosting business for the local tradespeople. At Reading Abbey they had a choice of 241 relics to venerate, including twenty-nine pertaining to Jesus, six to the Virgin Mary, nineteen to the patriarchs and prophets, fourteen to apostles, seventy-three to martyrs, fifty-one to confessors, and forty-nine to virgins.[2] Westminster could boast a vase containing some of Jesus' blood. Lincoln Cathedral, as well as housing the popular shrine of St Hugh, possessed a large number of other valuable relics including two fingers of Mary Magdalene. Bury St Edmunds, besides possessing the shrine of Edmund, the king martyr, could display the coals on which St Lawrence was roasted and Thomas of Canterbury's penknife and boots. Bath Abbey owned combs said to have belonged to Mary Magdalene, St Dorothy, and St Margaret.

Belief in the efficacy of physical contact with holy things impelled the devout to the most extraordinary excesses. They scooped up and even ate dust which had gathered on the tombs of the saints. They took away phials of water which had been used to wash the tombs. Twelfth-century visitors to Bury St Edmunds Abbey had to be restrained from biting off pieces of gilt from the shrine of the martyr. To the medieval mind, spiritual benefits could not only be conveyed *through* material objects, but could also assume material attributes. Gregory of Tours was, admittedly, writing in the sixth century, but there is no doubt that his attitude towards divine grace was one which was to become a permanent feature of popular piety until the Reformation. Gregory describes a pilgrim visiting the tomb of St Peter in Rome:

> *Should he wish to bring back a relic from the tomb, he*
> *carefully weighs a piece of cloth which he then hangs*
> *inside the tomb. Then he prays ardently and, if his faith*
> *is sufficient, the cloth, once removed from the tomb, will*
> *be found to be so full of divine grace that it will be much*
> *heavier than before. Thus will he know that his prayers*
> *have been granted.[3]*

Some church leaders warned against the crasser examples of materialism. As early as 813 the Second Council of Talons inveighed against the "simple-minded notion that sinners need only catch sight of the shrines of the saints and their sins will be absolved". Orthodox preachers and heretics in later years took up the cry. But they made little impact; the religion of the people took more comfort in the tangible, traditional objects of devotion than in the abstract subtleties of the theologians. What Johan Huizinga pointed out in the early twentieth century remains valid:

> *The spirit of the Middle Ages, still plastic and naïve,*
> *longs to give concrete shape to every conception. Every*
> *thought seeks expression in an image, but in this*
> *image it solidifies and becomes rigid. By this tendency*
> *to embodiment in visible forms all holy concepts are*
> *constantly exposed to the danger of hardening into mere*
> *externalism. For in assuming a definite figurative shape*
> *thought loses its ethereal and vague qualities, and pious*

feeling is apt to resolve itself in the image.[4]

It is not surprising to learn that popular Christian belief was liberally mixed with pagan survivals, folk religion, and magic. Those in poor health or other distress were as likely to resort to witches, wizards, healers, fortune-tellers, astrologers, and other practitioners of the occult as they were to their parish clergy. Spells cast by such agents of forbidden arts frequently aped church rituals, incorporated Christian prayers, and used holy water or consecrated wafers. In fact, most people found it difficult to differentiate between church magic and occult magic. If the priest at mass could "make God" by muttering a few Latin words over the Host, as the church taught, who was to say that a knife or a wand could not be similarly invested with spiritual power?

Clergy considered themselves, and were considered by their flocks, to be primarily performers of rituals rather than teachers of Christian truth. As late as 1551, Hooper, the bishop of Gloucester in the process of a visitation of his 311 clergy discovered that 168 could not remember all the Ten Commandments, thirty-three could not locate them in the Bible, ten were unable to recite the Lord's Prayer, and thirty-four did not know who its author was. For a hundred years or more, zealous bishops had complained about the educational inadequacy of priests, many of whom knew just about enough Latin to mutter their way through the mass. This state of affairs was perhaps understandable during the centuries when books were extremely expensive, hand-made objects, but the printing press had been invented a full century before Bishop Hooper made his disturbing discovery. His statistics can be backed up by others.

Between 1500 and 1550, 869 East Anglian clergy left wills which were proved in the consistory court at Norwich, the second city in the kingdom. Only 158 died possessed of any books at all. Of that residue fifty-eight clergy merely had service books (missals, manuals, processionaries, etc.) to bequeath. That leaves a round hundred who might have owned devotional, instructional, or apologetic works. No detailed information is given about twenty-one of the remaining clerical libraries. We are thus left with seventy-nine parish clergy about whose literary and religious tastes we can discern something. Most of them owned collections of sermons and anthologies of legends and stories of the "miraculous" type already mentioned. Twelve testators owned Latin Bibles. Thus, only a dozen pastors throughout a large, populous, and thriving part of England owned the sourcebook of the Christian faith. Fewer than a hundred possessed preaching aids and the vast majority were concerned only with the mechanical performance of their pastoral, ritual, and sacramental duties.

The Medieval Bible

What place, then, did the Christian Scriptures occupy in the life of the medieval English church? The only approved edition of the Bible was the Latin Vulgate, completed by St Jerome around 404. When it was first devised it had been a good piece of work, being based on the best Greek and Hebrew sources then available. But it had never succeeded, as was intended, in ousting the many versions of Scripture popular in different regions. So there had never been an undisputed common text. As centuries of painstaking manuscript-copying passed, variant readings had become incorporated in the Vulgate. Inevitably, errors crept in as the book was copied laboriously by hand.

The Vulgate was the standard text in the theology courses of Europe's great universities. There the schoolmen, the masters of exegesis and disputation, gathered their students around them and lectured on the chosen books of the sacred corpus. By the fourteenth century the full course lasted eight years and involved attending lectures, taking part in disputations, reading commentaries, delivering lectures, and becoming fully acquainted with the exegetical writings of the early church fathers and other great theologians. It would be reasonable to suppose that any scholar who survived this academic assault course would possess, not merely a doctorate, but a thorough knowledge of the Bible.

This was not always the case: the medieval universities turned out many excellent theologians with a firm grasp of God's redemptive plan as expounded in holy writ; they also turned out a multitude of mediocre minds stuffed to overflowing with Bible scraps.

Standards of teaching varied with the passing of the years and the arrival and departure of brilliant teachers, but that in itself does not explain the poor overall standard of biblical scholarship. One reason for this was over-reliance on the *glossae*. Many great doctors had produced notes or "glosses" on the biblical text and these had been collected and made into books. It was possible for students to accomplish a considerable part of their course with a knowledge only of the second-hand wisdom of the schoolmen. Similar to the *glossae* were the *Sentences*. These were collections of theological and doctrinal statements made by revered masters, the most popular being the *Sentences* of Peter Lombard. The opinions of this twelfth-century doctor were soon accepted as orthodox and as required reading for all theological students. Throughout the medieval period the *Sentences* enjoyed a place second only to the Bible as a repository of divine revelation. In practice students were often more familiar with Peter Lombard's work than with Scripture. It is always easier to trot out a fashionable scholar's ideas than to go back to the original.

Not only was an orthodox interpretation of Scripture forced on students by means of the *glossae* and the *Sentences*, but standard techniques of exposition tended to obscure the meaning. Any passage of the Bible which did not have an obvious reference to its medieval readers was gilded with symbolism or allegorized to give it spiritual significance. For example, this is how readers of the *Glossa Ordinaria*, the standard medieval commentary, were bidden to interpret the building of Noah's ark:

> *Now the fact that the ark is six times as long as it is broad and ten times as long as it is deep presents an exact likeness with the human body in which Christ was made manifest. For the length of a body from the crown of the head to the sole of the foot is six times the*

breadth, that is to say from one side to the other, and it is ten times its height, that is the measurement from the back to the belly. Then, the broad expanse of fifty cubits symbolizes the manner in which the heart expands under the influence of that love which the Holy Ghost inspires, as the apostle said: "the love of God hath been shed forth in our hearts". For it was on the fiftieth day after the Resurrection that Christ sent forth the Holy Spirit which expanded the hearts of the faithful. Now a length of three hundred cubits amounts to six times fifty, and in the same way the whole extent of time falls into six ages, in which Christ was proclaimed without ceasing: in the fifth he is the subject of prophecy, while in the sixth he is openly proclaimed in the Gospel.[5]

Sections of the Vulgate were incorporated into the mass. There were readings from the Gospels and epistles; the psalms were chanted; and many other parts of the service were direct quotations from or adaptations of Scripture. But all this was of little value to people who understood no Latin. Parishioners came and went during the celebration and, after leaving church, devoted the rest of the Sunday or feast day to pursuits which, if some grumblers are to be believed, were less than edifying. In 1362 no less a person than Archbishop Simon Islip of Canterbury (d. 1366) said that holy days,

> *... are now turned to blasphemy, seeing that assemblages, trading and other unlawful pursuits are specially followed upon these days; that which was prepared as a summary of devotion is made into a heap of dissipation, since upon these holy-days the tavern is rather worshipped than the Church, gluttony and drunkenness are more abundant than tears and prayers, men are busied rather with wantonness and contumely than with the leisure of contemplation.[6]*

However, whatever state of ignorance simple English men and women found themselves in, their literate neighbours of an enquiring turn of mind were not totally devoid of all knowledge of the Bible in their native tongue. Translations and interpretations existed of some passages of Scripture. There were three types of vehicle which conveyed parts of the sacred text into the common stream of consciousness: poetry, *glossae*, and straight translation. Caedmon, a seventh-century monk of Whitby Abbey, was, according to Bede, a simple cowherd before he took the cowl, but the gift of poetry was miraculously bestowed upon him and he used it to sing the praises of God and to retell in popular form the great Bible stories. The medium of verse paraphrase was used by later poets such as Cynewulf and the author of one of the masterpieces of Old English literature, *The Dream of the Rood*.

Such orthodox translations as existed grew out of the *glossae*. In many biblical texts, such as the *Lindisfarne Gospels*, the interlinear commentaries were in the vernacular. Some of them were scholarly comments on the original but others were word-for-word translations. They were used within the monasteries for instructing novices and schoolchildren. Like other *glossae*, some of these interpolations were collected and bound separately. This was particularly true of the psalter (the book of Psalms), which was the most important part of the Bible for liturgical and devotional use. Many versions of the psalms, in prose and verse form, were in circulation by the end of the medieval period. There were also extant translations of Genesis and the Gospels available to the literate devout.

All these vernacular fragments came into existence despite, rather than because of, official ecclesiastical policy. Notwithstanding its acknowledged shortcomings and the fact that there was no single version accepted throughout western Christendom, church leaders adopted a fundamentalist attitude towards the canon of the Vulgate. It was inspired by God and could not be altered. It was in Latin, the immaculate language of the classical world, of Augustine, Jerome, and the early doctors of the western church, a language spoken by some of the apostles themselves. The very idea of debasing it by rendering it into "marketplace English" was, to many, abhorrent. And what could possibly be the purpose of making the Bible available in the common tongue? Reformers claimed that it would be easier for priests and people to understand the things of God, but how could this be? Did it not take eight years of hard study for a scholar to become acquainted with the deep mysteries of redemption? If the uneducated laity could read the Bible, they would not be able to understand it. What would be worse, they might think that they did understand it. That would be dangerous; that path led to heresy. No, it was not necessary for common people to have the Bible; God had decreed that they should achieve salvation by good works and by such acts of piety as they were directed towards by their spiritual superiors. It was for the church to mediate to the people the grace of God in word and sacrament, which would empower them and inspire them to holiness of living. More perceptive ecclesiastics had another reason for opposing translation into the vernacular: they realized that translation implied interpretation. In choosing modern words approximating to the Latin originals, any translator would be inadvertently imposing his own prejudices and opinions on the church.

Yet there were always some people who wanted to know more. In every generation there appeared devout men and women, clergy and lay, who could not be satisfied with conventional religion. Some availed themselves of the pathway laid down by the church for those who sought a rigid pattern of devotion. They entered the cloistered world of the monastery or nunnery. Others joined guilds or brotherhoods which maintained altars or chantry chapels and administered local charities. Some banded together to perform religious music or to enact biblical stories on portable public stages. There were those who sought the mystic or ascetic path, living in seclusion to devote themselves to prayer and who gained a reputation as holy men and women.

One proof of widespread lay devotion is the large number of primers that have survived. These illustrated books of psalms and prayers designed for personal use began to circulate as soon as printing began in the mid-fifteenth century. They encouraged people to learn to read, although doubtless illiterate buyers acquired them so that their better educated friends and relatives could read them aloud for their edification. It was only a matter of time before pious souls clamoured to possess their own Bibles.

Church authorities were uncertain about the spread of lay devotion. As long as it was directed into conventional channels, all was well. But pious men and women could get above themselves. When they manifestly lived purer lives or understood the faith better than their priests, members of the establishment felt challenged. They smelled HERESY.

Chapter 2

The English Heresy

In 1401 the bishops succeeded in getting Parliament to create a new statute, *De Heretico Comburendo*. It revived an old law and provided that when an individual had been found guilty of heresy by church courts, the king's officers

> *shall receive, and them before the people in an high place cause to be burnt, that such punishment may strike fear into the minds of others, whereby no such wicked doctrine and heretical and erroneous opinions, against the Catholic faith, Christian law, and determination of the holy church ... be sustained or in any way suffered; ...*[1]

It was, of course, the ecclesiastical establishment who decided what was and what was not heresy, and in 1408 Archbishop Arundel (1353–1414) convened a conference at Oxford in which a draconian set of laws was formulated defining very closely what activities the bishops had in mind. Article VII of these Constitutions of Oxford pronounced a total veto on lay access to vernacular Scripture, "under pain of excommunication and the stigma of heresy".

> *We resolve therefore and ordain that no one henceforth on*
> *his own authority translate any text of Holy Scripture*
> *into the English or any other language by way of a book,*
> *pamphlet or tract, and that no book, pamphlet or tract*
> *of this kind... be read in part or in whole, publicly or*
> *privately, under pain of the great excommunication, until*
> *the translation shall have been approved by the diocesan*
> *of the place, or if need be by a provincial council.*

The bishops justified their ban as follows:

> *It is a perilous thing, as the Blessed Jerome testifies,*
> *to translate the text of Holy Scripture from one idiom*
> *into another, inasmuch as in the translations themselves*
> *it is no easy matter in all cases, as the Blessed Jerome,*
> *albeit inspired, confesses that he often went astray in this*
> *respect.*[2]

This succinctly stated the dilemma that would trouble all translators in succeeding centuries. It was an important technical point, but behind it lay the issue of authority. Arundel and his colleagues believed that the church (which, in this case, meant the clergy) held the monopoly of divine truth. The Vulgate buttressed Catholic doctrine. Opening up the thousand-year-old text to re-examination might appear to call in question what the church decreed to be truth. It could only *appear* to be a threat because there was no question of church and Bible being in conflict. But men equipped with the open Bible who had not been securely founded in Catholic teaching might come up with all manner of anarchic ideas. They were, in fact, already doing so, as a result of the pestilential preaching in Oxford a quarter of a century earlier of the arch-heretic, John Wycliffe.

John Wycliffe

Wycliffe was a brilliant academic born in Yorkshire about 1330. He spent most of his life at Oxford University and his career followed a conventional course. He graduated as an MA and was elected to a fellowship. In 1360 he became Master of Balliol but resigned this post the next year on being appointed to the fat benefice of Gillingham, Lincolnshire. He merely used his stipend to further his studies in theology. He now enjoyed a reputation as a brilliant lecturer and disputant in the philosophy schools. Other ecclesiastical appointments followed. His fame extended beyond the walls of the university and he became a fourteenth-century celebrity.

Leading academics have always attracted the attention of the government of the day and there were those at the court of the elderly Edward III who had their eyes on Master Wycliffe. The king was in his dotage and effective power vacillated between a clerical party headed by William of Wykeham, bishop of Winchester, and a group led by John of Gaunt, duke of Lancaster, which represented most of the nobility. In the long-running political conflict between the temporal and spiritual powers the former was currently in the ascendant. John of Gaunt, a seasoned warrior, enjoyed popular support and was able to appeal to English nationalism against the interference of Rome in domestic affairs and particularly at the imposition of high church taxes. In his search for propaganda support John of Gaunt naturally looked to the more radical thinkers of the day, and none was more radical than John Wycliffe.

In his lectures this Oxford scholar attacked the wealth and corruption of the clergy, in particular the monastic orders, and contrasted them with the poverty and purity of Jesus. He challenged the temporal power claimed by the church, rejected papal exactions, and asserted the supremacy of the civil power in all matters of property and criminal law. In 1374 he was appointed to the parish church of Lutterworth and a few weeks later he was sent to Bruges as part of an English delegation to discuss the issue of papal "provisions" (namely the appointment of men to English benefices by the pope). The granting of such posts to foreign clergy who never even entered the country, let alone visited their parishes, was a prime cause of discontent. Four years later the spiritual leadership of Christendom lost much of its credibility with the opening up of the Great Schism. From 1378 to 1417 two and sometimes three popes and antipopes contended for leadership of western Christendom. They were backed by rival groups of cardinals based in Rome, Avignon, and Pisa. The vicious squabbling between "holy fathers" who did not baulk at simony, bribery, and murder in their quest for power brought the papacy to its lowest ebb. The clamour for church reform in England now grew louder and Wycliffe was its leading theological spokesman. His own thinking moved on steadily during the 1370s. 1378 is a key date. That was when Wycliffe stated, in *De Officio Regis*,

> *It is not deducible from Scripture that the Pope's secular power extends over the temporal property of our realm.*[3]

Probably he did not appreciate when he wrote those words that he was headlining a revolutionary manifesto. To claim that the leadership of the church was in conflict with the church's foundation document was shatteringly outrageous. The Bible had always been there as a spur to morality, an aid to devotion, and a corrective to doctrinal error. It had inspired periodic holiness movements, such as that of St Francis, who had urged believers to espouse poverty in emulation of Jesus. But the majority of people who had access to Scripture were establishment men who took it as axiomatic that the Bible, properly understood, was always in support of current ecclesiastical teaching and practice. The party line was that only those could understand the word of God who had been through the educational mill and emerged as men whose opinions had been shaped by the process. The rare individuals (some consigned to the stake, others reckoned in later years to be saints) who presumed to use Scripture to back unconventional ideas were carefully watched by the authorities and usually silenced without too much difficulty. What made Wycliffe such a nuisance was that he had powerful protectors. By 1377 his sermons and lectures had already attracted

critical attention. Some of his teachings had been condemned by
Pope Gregory XI and he was on more than one occasion summoned
before his ecclesiastical superiors. But he had so much government
backing that his position was secure. Parliament supported his
anti-papal stand. And he enjoyed the active patronage of John
of Gaunt's party, which was now ruling the country in the name
of the young new king, Richard II. Beyond these, Wycliffe had a
rapidly growing number of followers among the common people.
When he appeared to answer charges before Bishop Courtenay of
London in 1377 the meeting was disrupted and eventually broken
up by Wycliffe's more unruly supporters.

But Wycliffe was no mere political tool of the aristocratic
establishment. His brilliant and enquiring mind could not be held
in check. The closer he studied the Bible, the more he drew logical
conclusions from what he read. In 1381 he claimed that, if the
Bible was the only authority in matters of faith, "all Christians, and
lay lords in particular, ought to know holy writ and to defend it".
If the pope persisted in maintaining existing unscriptural doctrines
and corrupt practices then he must be the Antichrist.

Now the government's star performer was beginning to
become an embarrassment. There was no doubt that Wycliffe had
wandered – or, rather, marched purposefully – into heresy. John
of Gaunt tried to persuade him to tone down his attack on the
Catholic hierarchy, but there was no shifting the Oxford scholar.
To make matters worse, the 1381 Peasants' Revolt, a spontaneous
expression of social and economic grievances, now broke out.
There was little or no connection between Wycliffite doctrines and
this desperate uprising of the people, but this timely eruption was
too good an opportunity for Wycliffe's enemies to miss. They could
and did claim that challenging spiritual authority inevitably led to
the breakdown of law and order. The political tables were now
turned on Lancaster's party and life became impossible for the
reformer at Oxford. He withdrew to his parish at Lutterworth.

But that did not mean that he abandoned his convictions or
even kept a low profile. The Bible had taken possession of his
mind. His intellectual struggle had brought him a new religious

freedom under a new authority – the word of God, written. He devoted the last few years of his life to the realization of his vision that "all Christians ought to know holy writ". For that, two things were necessary – copies of the Bible in English and preachers able to proclaim its message.

The Lollard Bible 1382–1500

The making of the first complete English Bible had been begun at Oxford in about 1380. For many years Wycliffe had been deterred by the sheer monumentality of rendering all the canonical and apocryphal books into English. What seems to have finally nerved him for the task was increasing popular demand. Wycliffe's disciples had been going out from Oxford armed with vernacular Gospels and other scraps of Scripture and the response was dramatic. People could not get enough of the sacred writings. So Wycliffe and a small group of trusted companions settled to the task, which would change England for ever.

The laborious work of translation was made more arduous by the need for secrecy; the translators could not refer too openly to the Latin grammars and other authorities they needed for their task. Yet so important was the work that they were not tempted to hurry or, driven by impatience, to take short cuts. Five men were involved in the new version and they handled the sacred text of the Vulgate with great veneration. Each worked carefully on his appointed section, translating the Latin word for word, not presuming to change the word order, even when their scruples rendered the meaning obscure.

In the summer of 1382 the chancellor of the university carried out a great purge at Oxford. Teachers and students alike fled to their several places of origin and they took with them the new books which enshrined their faith – whole Bibles, New Testaments, copies of the Gospels, paraphrases of Old Testament books and translations of Wycliffe's controversial treatises. But even as these were being shown and read to astonished parents and wide-eyed villagers throughout England, a new Bible translation was being prepared.

Wycliffe and his amanuensis, John Purvey, were not happy with the slavishly literal existing version with its close following of Latin syntax. From his refuge at Lutterworth, Purvey now undertook a freer, more idiomatic translation from the Vulgate. In a prologue he tells how he set about the task:

> *A simple creature hath translated the Bible out of Latin into English. First, this simple creature had much travail, with divers fellows and helpers, to gather many old Bibles and other doctors and common glosses, and to make one Latin Bible some deal true; and then to study it anew, the text with the gloss and the other doctors as he might get... that helped full much in this work; the third time to counsel with old grammarians and old divines of hard words and hard sentences, how they might be best understood and translated; the fourth time to translate as he could to the sentence, and to have many good fellows and cunning at the correcting of the translation.*[4]

It was obviously a long and laborious undertaking and one which involved many active minds. When the pioneer reformer died of a paralytic stroke on the last day of 1384, the task was passed on to others. Purvey seems to have moved from Lutterworth to Bristol where there was an active Wycliffite cell, in order to continue his work there. His revision was completed about 1388.

The bishops could not, of course, ignore this challenge. At first they used their pulpits to denounce the radicals. In 1382 Henry Crump, a Cistercian monk, preached against the Wycliffites from the pulpit of St Mary's, Oxford. He called their evangelists "lollards" or "lollers", using a familiar expression applied to heretical lay preachers in the Low Countries and derived from a Flemish word meaning to "mumble" or "mutter". The Wycliffites, according to their detractors, were men who "learn the gospels by heart in the vernacular and mumble the one to the other".[5]

It was the failure of conventional repressive measures which led to the enactment of *De Heretico Comburendo* and the Constitutions of Oxford. Taking advantage of their enhanced powers, the bishops carried out a wholesale purge of Lollards. Many were arrested and forced to recant. Some went to the stake rather than compromise their faith. As for the arch-heretic himself, death did not deliver him from the hatred of his enemies. In 1428 a ceremony, whose solemnity barely concealed its essential absurdity, took place at Lutterworth. A group of dark, robed figures stood around a grave in the churchyard while burly peasants dug down to the coffin. When Wycliffe's body had been exhumed the dignitaries seized his bones and burned them on a hastily built bonfire. When there was nothing of the great heretic left on earth but a pile of ashes, these were scattered in a nearby stream.

The bishops might well have felt confident that Lollardy had been scotched, that the entire movement had petered out in failure and ignominy. However, any congratulations they allowed themselves soon proved premature. In several parts of southern and central England groups of Lollards met secretly in towns and villages to read or listen to readings of Scripture and to consider their contemporary application. Most of them came from the class of skilled, literate traders and craftsmen. They were masons, carpenters, wool merchants, and leatherworkers – men and women whose work took them long distances in search of employment or markets. Where they went their beliefs and their Bibles went with them.

Although Lollardy had a few traditional strongholds, such as the Chilterns and central Kent, it was an amorphous phenomenon, difficult to detect and control. When apprehended, heretics usually denied their beliefs or recanted, only to continue their meetings afterwards with greater discretion. A Lollard convicted in one area might turn up again years later, hundreds of miles away, still spreading his poisonous doctrines. Some Lollard cells never came to the attention of the authorities because the local clergy regarded them as nothing more than groups of harmless cranks, who, whatever their beliefs, made no trouble and attended mass faithfully.

A glimpse through the very incomplete episcopal records of heresy proceedings gives us a fragmentary but clear picture of what the authorities were up against. Robert Silkeby of Coventry was a colporteur of Bibles and tracts. He travelled over a wide area obtaining the precious manuscripts by whatever means he could. On one occasion, he exchanged a bed for a Bible. For eighteen years he carried on his business unmolested, disseminating Bibles and tracts discreetly to the faithful. When at last he was brought before the bishops' court, he was forced on pain of death to reveal the names of other members of the sect together with the hiding places they used for their sacred writings. John Claydon was first arrested on suspicion of heresy in North Wales. He escaped conviction on that occasion, but twenty years later we find him in London where his home was one of the main Lollard centres and a factory for the manufacture of tracts and Bibles. He was busily proselytizing and indoctrinating new converts against the agents of "papistical anti-christ" when ecclesiastical justice eventually caught up with him. In 1415 Claydon was burned with several of his books at Smithfield. At Stanton in Leicestershire the village priest, Master Kent, was infected with heresy, for he had bought Lollard books from Dr Abcock, a physician from Ibstock. And in 1428 an informant deposed against Margery Baxter of Martham, Norfolk, that Margery "secretly desired her, that she and Joan her maid would come secretly, in the night, to her chamber, and there she should hear her husband read the law of Christ unto them, which law was written in a book that her husband was wont to read to her by night".[6]

Few Lollards went as far as to court arrest and execution. The majority were, to all outward appearances, devout, law-abiding Catholics who went to church, had their confessions heard by their parish priests, and did not draw attention to themselves by proselytizing. When arrested, they readily recanted − and then went on reading their Bibles in secret. Their approach to Scripture was non-controversial. They believed that the gospel truths were self-evident and needed no argument to drive them home. With a very few exceptions, no Lollards were revolutionaries. Wycliffe himself had ordered that the Bible was to be studied for edification only, not for controversy, curiosity, or the winning of a scholarly reputation. Christians should:

> ... *read busily the text of the New Testament, and take*
> *they example of the holy life of Christ, and of His*
> *apostles, and trust they fully to the goodness of the Holy*
> *Ghost, which is the special teacher of well-willed men...*
> *They should see and study the true and open exposition*
> *of holy doctors, and other wise men, as they may easily*
> *see as goodly come thereto. Let Christian men travail*
> *faithfully in these six ways, and be not too much afeared*
> *of objections of enemies, saying that "the letter slayeth".*[7]

Lollard tracts were, indeed, frequently polemical, but their presentations of Scripture always followed the guidelines laid down by their founder. Glosses and prefaces were never vehemently anti-establishment but were provided solely as aids to study and often incorporated quotations from the early church fathers.

In one of their tracts, *A proper dyaloge between a Gentillman and a husbandman*, the humble peasant succeeds in persuading his superior of the truth of Lollard doctrines until the gentleman acknowledges,

> *Now I promise thee after my judgement*
> *I have not heard of such an old fragment*
> *Better grounded on reason with Scripture.*
> *If such ancient things might come to light*
> *That noble men had once of them a sight*
> *The world yet would change peradventure.*[8]

Scripture and reason. These were the twin pillars on which Lollard teachings were based. Wycliffite disciples affirmed that nothing was necessary for salvation but the Bible, interpreted in a straightforward way without recourse to arcane, allegorical glosses. This is why Lollardy lacked many of the marks of other heretical sects. There was no "Lollard creed" or "Lollard priesthood" or "Lollard hierarchy". It may be that we are wrong to think of Lollardy as a specific heresy. What we are dealing with is a loose network of people who had discovered a secret and were trying to build their lives upon it. The exclusive knowledge they shared was that God revealed himself directly to his people via the Scriptures and without any need for clerical intermediaries. The Lollards were "people of the book" in a very specific sense. They identified with and were identified by the Bible. Reginald Pecock, a mid-fifteenth- century bishop of Chichester who took great pains to investigate and understand these radicals, discovered that "they give a name proper to themselves and call themselves '*known men*', as though all other than them be unknown".[9] This exclusive network of Bible devotees survived periodic persecution for well over a century, meeting for secret "night schools", frequently marrying "within the faith", and passing down their precious handwritten books to the next generation of "known men".

Their more determined enemies found them infuriating to deal with. The autonomous nature of Lollard cells, their efficient colportage system, the false recantations of those hauled before the courts, and their information networks made them impervious to conventional techniques of repression. Like quicksilver, they slipped through their accusers' fingers and easily regrouped. The medieval church could find no final solution to the Lollard problem. The fate of Reginald Pecock bears witness to the frustration felt by the authorities. Bishop Pecock was a remarkably sensitive and intelligent orthodox apologist. Instead of condemning the Lollards out of hand, he preferred to understand their beliefs and to counteract them by argument and citation from vernacular Scripture. Such an attitude smacked so much of dangerous toleration that Pecock himself was accused of heresy, forced to resign his bishopric, and imprisoned at Thorney Abbey. When even bishops could be ruined for their too great familiarity with the English Bible, mere laymen dedicated to religious freedom were likely to run the same risks.

Thus, long before the invention of the printing press, there were vernacular Bibles and Bible fragments circulating in England and a community of people dedicated to studying them. The Lollards were a tiny minority of the population but many of their neighbours, untainted by heresy, shared their discontent with the conventional church and were unconvinced about some of the doctrines they were supposed to believe. If ever the time came when vernacular Scriptures were widely available, there would be a ready market for them.

Erasmus and Luther

The next episode in our story begins in 1516 and its hero is another academic. The Dutchman Desiderius Erasmus (1466–1536) was a wandering scholar and an international celebrity. He was one of the prime movers of the literary Renaissance and had produced new editions of long-lost Latin classics. He was most famous for his runaway bestseller, *In Praise of Folly* (1508), a brilliant satire on contemporary society which did not spare the personnel and practices of the church. Between 1511 and 1514 he was in Cambridge, lecturing on Greek language and literature. The new university syllabus embraced the Renaissance rediscovery of classical studies and it was there that Erasmus embarked on his most revolutionary project, the *Novum Instrumentum*, published in 1516. It consisted of a fresh Greek text of the New Testament accompanied by a Latin translation. Erasmus studied the best early Greek versions he could find (most of them written in Constantinople in the early Middle Ages) and used them as the basis for a more accurate Latin text than the Vulgate. He brought to his work the enthusiasm and, perhaps, the naïvity of the pure scholar and believed that he was doing the church a service. He wanted to banish the obscurantism that prevailed in the theology schools and to direct scholars to the primary source, the Bible. And not only scholars. How is it, he wrote,

... that people give themselves so much trouble about the details of all sorts of remote philosophical systems and neglect to go to the sources of Christianity itself? ... wisdom... may be drawn from these few books, as from a crystalline source, with far less trouble than is the wisdom of Aristotle from so many thorny books and with much more fruit... The equipment for that journey is simple and at everyone's immediate disposal. This philosophy is accessible to everybody. Christ desires that his mysteries shall be spread as widely as possible. I should wish that all good wives read the Gospel and Paul's Epistles; that they were translated into all languages; that out of these the husbandman sang, while ploughing, the weaver at his loom; that with such stories the traveller should beguile his wayfaring. [10]

Erasmus's motivation was, in essence, the same as Wycliffe's: to cleanse the church of the moral, intellectual, and spiritual errors that were spoiling it, it was only necessary to direct the attention of Christian folk to the Bible. Traditionalists, who made up the majority of bishops, abbots, and university teachers, saw things very differently. For them the Vulgate was the inspired word of God. The church's doctrine had been based on it for more than a thousand years. Anyone challenging its accuracy was challenging the authority of Rome and must have heretical intent. How else could one explain Erasmus's exclusion of the Vulgate's proof text of the Trinity – "there are three that bear record in heaven, the Father, the Word and the Holy Ghost, and these three are one" (1 John 5:7–8)? Erasmus regarded this, correctly, as a later interpolation, not found in the best early manuscripts. Even more disturbing to the authorities was the scholar's rendition of the Greek *metanoeite* as "repent", rather than the official "do penance", which appeared to support the medieval sacramental system.

Nowhere did the *Novum Instrumentum* make more impact than in Cambridge, which became the intellectual home of the English Reformation. Erasmus himself comments, on a visit in December

1517, "Cambridge is a changed place, and this school detests those chill subtleties, which make more for disputation than for piety."[11] Interestingly, it was at this very time that a movement began in distant Saxony that would strike a very different note to Erasmus's urbane and witty critiques. In October 1517 a lecturer in the theology faculty of Wittenberg University protested at the practice of papal indulgences (spiritual rewards in the next world promised by the Catholic hierarchy in return for cash payments). Martin Luther's challenge began as little more than a respectful whisper, an invitation to fellow scholars to debate what the Bible had to say about indulgences and other church practices. Yet it, too, was but another example of Scripture being enlisted as a rival authority to Rome. The pope demanded Luther's recantation. Luther stubbornly refused, as he famously told the Emperor Charles V to his face, unless he could be proved wrong "by Scripture and plain reason". News of Luther's stand spread with astonishing rapidity, as did the numerous books he had printed to explain his beliefs. The whisper became a roar that was heard in all the towns and cities of Europe, including Cambridge.

William Tyndale

Early in 1521 the chancellor of the University of Cambridge ordered a public bonfire of all Luther's books before the west door of Great St Mary's Church. The proctor and his officers were busy for days searching students' rooms and ferreting out the forbidden volumes. They used bribery, force and threats in order to build a sufficiently large and impressive pyre. At the appointed time a large crowd in festive mood gathered to cheer as the vice chancellor with theatrical solemnity set a torch to the piled vellum and parchment. This was the signal for several radical students to flee Cambridge and the threat of persecution. One such was William Tyndale, a priest and theologian in his mid-twenties. He found a haven in the household of Sir John Walsh, a prominent Gloucestershire landowner, and was employed as tutor to his children. He was unable to keep quiet about the new ideas he had acquired at university. Unlike the old Lollards, many of the new breed of evangelicals felt the need to go on the offensive and Tyndale was soon in trouble for preaching in local churches what was contemptuously referred to as the "new learning". The young zealot concluded that it was "impossible to establish the lay people in any truth, except the Scripture were plainly laid before their eyes in their mother tongue". Within months he had dedicated himself to the task of translating the word of God into English.

The Constitutions of Oxford insisted that any translation had to have episcopal backing, so Tyndale went to London to seek the patronage of Bishop Cuthbert Tunstall. There was some reason for this, for Tunstall was known to be a humanist scholar in favour of cautious church reform. But he was no supporter of heretics. He had recently returned from a diplomatic mission to Germany, where he had witnessed, with alarm, the spread of Lutheranism. It is not, therefore, surprising that when Tyndale presented himself at the bishop's London house in July 1523, he was told there was no room for him in the household.

But Tyndale did find a patron. Through his preaching in St Dunstan's in the West, he came to the attention of the wealthy cloth merchant, Humphrey Monmouth. Monmouth was a member of London's heretical underworld; he was well known in Lollard circles, though his continental connections had brought him into contact with the more sophisticated Lutheranism. He was only too pleased to offer Tyndale money, food, and shelter. The city was a world in microcosm where, for the first time, Tyndale was able to observe the activities of political prelates and fashionable preachers, as well as the secret meetings of Lollards and Lutherans. What he saw did not please him but it did help him to reach an important decision.

> *I marked the course of the world, and heard our praters (I*
> *would say our preachers), how they boasted themselves and*
> *their high authority; and beheld the pomp of our prelates,*
> *and how busy they were, as they yet are, to set peace and*

*unity in the world (though it be not possible for them
that walk in darkness to continue long in peace, for they
cannot either but stumble or clash themselves at one thing
or another that shall clean unquiet all together), and saw
things whereof I defer to speak at this time, and understood
at the last not only that there was no room at my lord of
London's palace to translate the new Testament, but also
that there was no place to do it in all England...[12]*

In the spring of 1524 William Tyndale set sail for Germany and the one university town in Europe where he could be sure of finding an atmosphere favourable to his work – Luther's Wittenberg. He spent the best part of a year there labouring at the translation, aided by another exile, the ex-friar William Roy. He took Erasmus's Greek text, the *Novum Instrumentum*, as the basis of his translation. Though he was familiar with Luther's German Testament and, probably, with the Wycliffite Bible, his work was completely original. His own grasp of Greek was firm and assured, his theological understanding considerable. It was not enough for Tyndale simply to convey the words of Scripture from Greek into English; they had to be conveyed into living English, such as "a boy that driveth the plough" could understand. In this he was completely successful; his New Testament had a colloquial vigour, which rendered it immediately comprehensible and popular. Later translators found it impossible to improve on many of his renderings, which appeared in version after version down to the time of the King James Bible. Even today, Tyndale's rendering of the parable of the sower (Luke 8:5–8) strikes a familiar note:

*A sower went out to sowe his seed: and as he sowed,
some fell by the wayside, and it was trodden under feet,
and the fowls of the air devoured it up. And some fell on
stone, and as soon as it was sprung up, it withered away
because it lacked moistness. And some fell among thorns,
and the thorns sprang up with it and choked it. And
some fell on good ground, and sprang up and bare fruit*

an hundredfold. And as he said these things, he cried: He that hath ears to hear, let him hear.

By the middle of 1525 the translation was sufficiently far advanced for Tyndale to look for a printer. Probably on the advice of his backers, he decided to take the manuscript to Cologne, an important printing centre on the Rhine which had regular trading connections with London. There the presses of Peter Quentel were soon creaking busily on the pages of Matthew's Gospel. All was going well until John Cochlaeus paid a chance visit to the workshop. Cochlaeus was a formidable champion of the Roman Church and was engaged in a bitter pamphlet war with Luther. He overheard Quentel's workmen talking about the English book and was immediately on the alert. In order to loosen the men's tongues a little more, he took them to a nearby inn. Soon he knew the whole story and he wasted no time reporting it to the town authorities. But before the agents of officialdom could swoop, Tyndale and Roy had been warned. They hurried to the print works, collected the sheets already run off and hastened to the jetty. There they found a boat to take them up the Rhine to Worms. The city authorities here were sympathetic to the cause of reform and Tyndale soon found a printer, named Peter Schoeffer, who was prepared to complete the book.

As all authors know, it is one thing to write a book and quite another to sell it. That is where the marketing men come in. Tyndale had the backing of a group of entrepreneurs who were as bold as they were canny. The Christian Brethren, of whom Humphrey Monmouth was a member, were a group of evangelical businessmen who were determined to spread the word – literally – and who also knew that there was a profit in so doing. Their market research assured them that despite the ban on illegal translations, there was a huge demand for them. The writings of Luther and other continental reformers, as well as old Lollard tracts, sold out as soon as they could be shipped into England.

Thomas More, a friend of Erasmus but a staunch enemy of the new breed of evangelicals, was horrified by the smuggling of heretical books. He wrote:

> ... *though they neither can be there printed without great*
> *cost [nor] none there sold without great adventure and*
> *peril, yet they cease not with money sent from thence to*
> *print them there and send them hither by the whole vats*
> *full at once, and in some places looking for no lucre,*
> *cast them abroad by night... I was by good honest men*
> *informed that in Bristol... there were of these pestilent*
> *books some thrown in the streets and left at men's doors by*
> *night that where they durst not offer their poison to sell,*
> *they would of their charity poison men for naught.*[13]

Tyndale's financiers had confidently ordered a first printing of 6,000 copies. In the spring of 1526 the consignment was shipped down the Rhine and unloaded in the English trading house at Antwerp, the depot of the Merchant Adventurers. From there the books were sold in batches to English dealers and arrangements were made for their secret despatch to ports on the other side of the Channel.

In England the reaction was intense and immediate. The Christian Brethren had handled well their prepublication advertizing and everywhere men were waiting eagerly for the forbidden books, which filtered inland from London and the east coast ports. All sorts and conditions of men rushed to buy them. The Lollards of Steeple Bumpstead in Essex sent one of their number, John Tyball, to examine the New Testament offered for sale by Friar Robert Barnes in London, and to compare it with their own books:

> ... *certain old books they had: as of four Evangelists,*
> *and certain epistles of Peter and Paul in English. Which*
> *books the said friar did little regard, and made a twit of*
> *it, and said, "A point for them, for that they be not to be*
> *[compared with] the new printed Testament in English,*
> *for it is of more cleaner English".*[14]

Having urged the Essex man to "keep it close", Barnes sold him a New Testament for 3s 2d, which was probably more than Tyball earned in a week.

At Oxford the main agent was Thomas Garett. By the time of his arrest in February 1528 he had already distributed 350 books to members of the university. Nor was it only students and merchants who were vulnerable to the new influences. The highest in the land possessed and read Tyndale's translation. Only a few years later Queen Anne Boleyn possessed her own copy of the New Testament specially bound in vellum with her name, *Anna Regine Anglia* [sic], in red letters on the fore-edge. Furthermore, she was openly interceding for those suffering persecution for their part in propagating the new books:

> ... *we be credibly informed that the bearer hereof, Richard Herman, merchant and citizen of Antwerp... was in the time of the late lord cardinal put and expelled from his freedom and fellowship of and in our English house there, for nothing else... but only... that he did... help to the setting forth of the New Testament in English. We therefore desire and instantly pray you, with all speed and favour convenient, to cause this good and honest merchant... to be restored to the pristine freedom, liberty, and fellowship aforesaid...* [15]

The bishops had never been as alarmed as they were by the influx and spread of the new translation. Tunstall complained bitterly that many,

> ... *maintainers of Luther's sect, blinded through extreme wickedness, wandering from the way of truth and the Catholic faith, have craftily translated the New Testament into our English tongue, intermeddling there with many heretical articles and erroneous opinions... attempting by their wicked and perverse interpretations to profane the majesty of the Scriptures, which hitherto*

*have remained undefiled, and craftily to abase the most
holy word of God, and the true sense of the same, of
the which translation there are many books printed,
some with glosses, and some without, containing in the
English tongue that pestiferous and most pernicious poison
dispensed throughout all our diocese of London in great
numbers, which truly without it be speedily foreseen,
without doubt will contaminate and infect the flock
committed unto us, with most deadly poison and heresy.[16]*

Tyndale's Translations

The authorities had no little cause for alarm. Tyndale's biblical
texts were not simply translations of Scripture into English. As
Tunstall had complained, every one of them after 1526 carried
anti-Catholic glosses. Church leaders who had always insisted that
the Bible was too difficult for ordinary people to understand were
to a large degree right. The evangelical campaigners for translation
knew this. It therefore seemed obvious to them that the text needed
an expository commentary.

Tyndale, like Luther, turned the word of God into an evangelical
tract. He was not content to leave the reader to interact with
Scripture and make of it what he or she could. That really would
open the door to heresy. So he told the reader what to think. For
example, relating one of the brushes Jesus had with the Pharisees,
Tyndale did not explain who the Pharisees actually were. He
simply made it very clear who their hypocritical and power-seeking
equivalents were in the sixteenth-century world:

*The high prelates so defended the right of holy church,
and so feared [frightened] the people with the curse of
God and terrible pains of hell, that no man durst leave
the vilest herb in his garden untithed. And the offerings
and things dedicate unto God, for the benefit of his holy
vicars, were in such estimation and reverence, that it was*

*a much greater sin to swear... by them than... by God.
What vengeance then of God, and how terrible and
cruel damnation... preached they to fall on them that
had stolen so the holy things? And yet, saith Christ, that
righteousness and faith, in keeping promise, mercy and
indifferent judgement, were utterly trodden under foot, and
clean despised of these blessed fathers...[17]*

No one can have been in any doubt as to whom these words referred but to make absolutely sure Tyndale added a marginal note: "The false and wicked doctrine of the papists."

This is a good indication of how bitter the conflict between evangelicals and reactionaries had become in such a short space of time. Any academic fair-mindedness and courtesy Tyndale might once have extended to his opponents had been driven out by the arrogant opposition with which he had been met and the persecution unto death some of his spiritual brethren had been subjected to. He had developed a profound hatred, not only for individual foes, but for the entire church establishment which he considered to be the household of Antichrist and which, by sacerdotal confidence tricks, was preying on simple people. His assault provoked a literary response in the same violent vein from Thomas More, who accused him of using the Bible as a vehicle for peddling heresy. Here were two educated men who were regarded by friends and acquaintances as gentle and courteous in personal relationships but who became bigoted and unyielding in their attitudes to the Bible. For Tyndale the word of God was self-authenticating and stood in judgment on all men and all institutions. More espoused the establishment view that the Bible had to be interpreted by the church – i.e. the papal hierarchy. There could be no meeting of minds between these starkly opposed controversialists.

But the momentum lay with Tyndale and his Lutheran associates. The bishops went to prodigious lengths to remove Tyndale's work from circulation, even to the extent of buying up whole consignments in order to burn them. They were fighting a losing battle, as the commercial success of English Bibles clearly proved. Tyndale lived centuries before the invention of copyright laws and was powerless to stop the pirate versions of his work, which began to appear as early as 1526. That was the year in which Christopher and Hans van Endhoven made their own printing of the Tyndale Testament at Antwerp. The brothers were prodigious in their output; during the next decade they reprinted the book no fewer than fourteen times. Whether their overriding interest was religious or commercial we know not, but we do know that they persevered despite fierce opposition and serious setbacks. In 1527 the book was banned in Antwerp; in 1528 Hans was imprisoned in England; and in 1531 Christopher died in a cell at Westminster, but his widow kept the presses turning.

The battle of the Bible became increasingly bitter in the 1530s. Inevitably it came to be mixed up with Henry VIII's long-running conflict with the pope over his divorce from Catherine of Aragon (see pp. 48). The more the agents of Rome prevaricated, the more determined the king was to have his own way. The English Reformation, which gathered momentum throughout this troubled decade, was about much more than religion and certainly about much more than the vernacular Bible. But "free access to the word of God" was one of the banners under which evangelicals fought.

In his pamphlet *A Pathway into Holy Scripture* (1530) Tyndale described the gospel as "good, merry, glad and joyful tidings, that maketh a man's heart glad, and maketh him sing, dance, and leap for joy",[18] but in defence of and opposition to this gospel, men were anything but merry and carefree. The bishops threw people into prison for possessing the New Testament, burned those who persisted in their heresies, and forced others to flee abroad for safety.

Tyndale's principal haven was now Antwerp, though he travelled frequently to other north European towns. He wrote a number of books and pamphlets during the ensuing years, but his consuming passion was the Bible and he now turned his attention to the Old Testament. For this he had to master Hebrew, which he had almost certainly not studied in England. He began his learning of the language at Wittenberg and persevered with it throughout the troubled years that followed. Early in 1529 he completed the Pentateuch, the first five books of the Bible, and decided to print it as a separate volume at Hamburg. By May 1530 his translation of the opening books of the Bible was in print. The next year he followed it with a translation of the book of Jonah. This was destined to be his last contribution to the English Bible.

The tide of persecution now moved closer to the translator himself, for in this same year, Humphrey Monmouth and Tyndale's brother John were arrested. Both abjured after a short spell in prison. Monmouth, because of his importance as an alderman of the City of London, was spared further humiliation, but John Tyndale was paraded through the streets of the capital sitting backwards on a horse with New Testaments draped around him and a placard stating, "I have sinned against the King".

However, William Tyndale continued with his mission. Most of his time was spent revising his earlier translation. His 1534 edition of the New Testament contained about 4,000 changes to the text but it was much more than a corrected version of the earlier New Testament. It contained marginal glosses, a preface "W. T. unto the Reader", and introductions to each individual book. The combination of good, clear text and evangelical commentary made this 1534 edition the most effective and popular weapon in the reformers' armoury. It was sold out within weeks and at the turn of the year another edition appeared, containing a few more minor revisions.

Even when allowance is made for the large numbers of New Testaments which were confiscated it is obvious that by 1535 there were several thousand copies of the book circulating in England and that they were to be found in the humblest dwellings as well as the manor houses of the realm. In 1537 Edward Fox, bishop of Hereford, could galvanize an assembly of his brother bishops by telling them, "The lay people know the Scriptures better than many of us." All but the most bigoted of the diocesans had to admit that this was true and that the policy of repression had dismally failed to prevent the spread of the English New Testament. Attempts to muzzle the Scriptures were counterproductive. When authority censors books, it makes many people wonder what it is trying to hide. More than that, it arouses in many the suspicion that they are being denied their birthright. One of the many anonymous tracts of the day asserted,

> ... it is proved lawful, that both men and women lawfully may read and write God's law in their mother tongue, and they that [forbid] this, show themselves heirs and sons of the first tormentors, and worse; for they show themselves the very disciples of Antichrist, which hath and shall pass all the malice of tyrants that have been before, in stopping and perverting of God's law; which deed engendereth great vengeance to fall in this realm, [unless] it be amended. For Paul saith, "The wrath of God is showed from heaven upon cruelness and unrighteousness of those men that withhold the truth of God."[19]

Such protests were only expressed by a minority but that minority was influential in the social circles of court and capital. It would eventually force the hand of government.

Tyndale, however, would not live to see it. Though necessarily cautious, he had a naïvely trusting nature. In May 1535 he was betrayed into the hands of his enemies. He was seized and marched off to the castle of Vilvorde, near Antwerp.

Tyndale remained in prison for exactly 500 days. We are given only one glimpse of him during that time but it is a very moving one. It takes the form of an appeal addressed to the Marquis of Bergen as the winter of 1535–36 drew on:

> I believe, most illustrious sir, that you are not unaware of what has been decided concerning me. I therefore beg your lordship, and that by the Lord Jesus, that if I am to stay

*here through the winter, you will ask the officer to be good
enough to send me from my goods which he has, a warmer
cap. I suffer greatly from cold in the head, and have a
perpetual catarrh, which is made worse in this cell. A
warmer coat too, for the one I have is very thin, and also
a piece of cloth to patch up my leggings. My overcoat is
worn out, and so are my shirts. He has a woollen shirt
of mine, if he will be good enough to send it. Also he
has my leggings of thicker material to go on top, and my
warmer night cap. I am making request to be allowed a
lamp in the evening, for it is tedious sitting alone in the
dark. But most of all I earnestly entreat and implore you
to ask the officer to allow me my Hebrew Bible, Hebrew
Grammar and Hebrew Dictionary so that I may spend
my time in those studies. And in return may you be
granted your greatest desire, so long as it is consistent with
the salvation of your soul. But if, before the winter is over,
any other decision has been made about me, I shall be
patient, abiding the will of God to the glory of the grace
of my Lord Jesus Christ, whose Spirit, I pray, may ever
direct your heart. Amen.*[20]

Was he allowed his precious books or did he have to console
himself through the cold days and nights with prayer and
meditation? We do not know. What we do know is that on the
morning of 6 October 1536 William Tyndale was led from his
cell to the nearby place of execution. The crowd, among whom
there must have been some of his Antwerp friends, were moved
to pity mingled with admiration as the shabby and dishevelled
figure walked with a firm and dignified step towards the pile of
faggots. The end was mercifully quick, the executioner strangling
the condemned man at the stake before the fire was kindled.

Thirteen years before, Tyndale had set himself the task of
translating the whole Bible into English. He had not accomplished
that task but in no sense of the word can he be said to have failed.
The cause had now claimed its most celebrated martyr and

Tyndale's fate inspired others to carry on the battle. According to legend the translator's last words were, "Lord, open the king of England's eyes." His friends and admirers in court circles were well placed to be agents for the granting of that prayer.

CHAPTER 3

"LET IT GO OUT AMONG OUR PEOPLE"

The story of the English Bible in the sixteenth century is tangled and dramatic because the sixteenth century was dramatic and tangled. Henry VIII's long struggle to escape from his first marriage led to the severing of the English church from papal obedience and the proclamation of Henry as supreme head of the church. The king had not hesitated to bid for support from Protestant states on the continent but there was no clear indication how far he was prepared to lead the nation along the Reformation path. Would he sanction the translation of the Bible? Would he allow all his subjects to read it? During the brief reign of his young son, Edward VI (1547–53), England veered sharply towards the evangelical cause, only to have the clock put back by Queen Mary (1553–58). Not until the closing years of the reign of Elizabeth I (1558–1603) did England become a defiant Protestant nation whose ruler was excommunicated and whose enemies were determined to bring it back into the Catholic fold by if necessary, conquests, and internal subversion, and political assassination.

As the nation lurched back and forth it became bitterly divided, not only between Catholics and Protestants, but also between traditionalist and radical groups within the English church. Inevitably, there were some who wanted the Reformation to go further and those who thought that it had already gone too far. All these tensions were reflected in the history of the English Bible.

The first versions of vernacular Scripture to receive the seal of royal approval emerged from the obscuring smoke and flame of violent and tragic conflict which mark the mid-1530s as one of the most turbulent in English history. The direction of religious policy lay largely in the hands of Thomas Cromwell, the king's secretary, whom the king nominated as his Vicegerent in Spirituals (effectively his representative in church affairs), and Thomas Cranmer, the archbishop of Canterbury Henry had put in place to grant him his divorce. Both men were reformers. Henry's second wife, Anne Boleyn, was also well disposed to religious change and used her patronage to install radical bishops and preachers. The dominant faction at court was, thus, behind rapid change. But courtiers and even queens could fall as suddenly as they had risen when a king like Henry VIII was on the throne. His long struggle for the divorce, his deteriorating health, and his lack of money turned him from a self-willed despot into an unpredictable tyrant with violent mood swings. He was ready to sacrifice anyone who resisted his demands – and those demands fluctuated.

As far as religious policy was concerned, he was in a dilemma. He prided himself on being a Renaissance prince and a patron of humanistic studies (he was an admirer of Erasmus and tried to entice Europe's leading intellectual back to England). He also wanted to be seen as a good Catholic and staunch enemy of heretics. He saw his country splitting into rival camps and was genuinely worried about the disunity (which he himself had done much to provoke). By 1530 it was clear that the bishops were powerless to prevent the spread of Tyndale's translations and Lutheran tracts. One pragmatic solution, urged upon him by the leaders of reform, was to sanction a new official Bible, free of damaging heretical glosses. In May he laid the problem on his bishops' shoulders: they were to come up with a fresh translation. That was a recipe for inaction. The conservative prelates dragged their feet and, by 1535, Cranmer was complaining that it would be doomsday before they produced anything.

They were profoundly uneasy about the impact of an open Bible because it would place in the hands of every literate man and woman a yardstick with which to measure the actions of their superiors in church and state. Thomas More dismissed the idea that "we should believe nothing but plain Scripture" as a "pestilential heresy". It could only lead to every reader becoming his or her own theologian. Such potentially boundless diversity of view would be intolerable. "I pray God," he confided to his son-in-law,

> *that some of us, high as we seem to sit upon the*
> *mountains treading heretics under our feet like ants, live*
> *not in the day that we gladly would wish to be at a league*
> *and composition with them, to let them have their churches*
> *quietly to themselves, so that they would be content to let*
> *us have ours quietly by ourselves.*[1]

Religious toleration was inconceivable to the sixteenth-century mind. Freedom of belief was like gunpowder placed beneath the walls of the bastion state. The initiative was left with the reformers. Since Henry had declared himself, theoretically, in favour of a new translation, Cromwell, Cranmer, and their friends were able to go ahead with their own plans. The result was not one but two texts of Scripture – Coverdale's Bible (1535) and "Matthew's" Bible (1537).

Miles Coverdale

Miles Coverdale (1488–1568) was an ex-friar who had spent some time with Tyndale and his team of scholars and printers. Coverdale worked with his English friend in Hamburg and moved with him to Antwerp, where they were supported by their co-religionists in the Low Countries, many of whom belonged to the wealthy trading community. One such merchant was Jacob van Meteren, who made frequent journeys across the southern North Sea to England. His declared cargoes were wool, cloth, and wine but his bales and casks often concealed smuggled New Testaments. By the mid-1530s the English Bible had become the hottest property in the world of European publishing and van Meteren urged Coverdale to produce a version which would be more commercially viable than what Tyndale had in mind. He knew that Tyndale's outspoken glosses would never win approval. There was, van Meteren urged, a good chance that an unglossed English Bible would be allowed into the country and might even obtain the royal licence. Either way there was little doubt that the Bibles would enjoy a wide sale. It was a classic example of the twin Protestant virtues of holy zeal and good business.

Coverdale completed the work in an astonishingly short space of time. As each section came from his pen it was rushed to the printers for setting. Van Meteren commissioned a title page from the English court painter, Hans Holbein. By 4 October 1535 the task was finished and the first batch of Bibles were stacked neatly in van Meteren's warehouse awaiting shipment to England. As a piece of translation, Coverdale's first Bible was not in the same class as Tyndale's. The Yorkshire priest was no classical linguist and he did not start from the original Greek and Hebrew texts, his version being based on the Vulgate, Tyndale's work, the Zürich Bible, Luther's German translation, and Santi Pagnini's Latin edition of 1528. Nevertheless, while Coverdale may have used a ragbag of sources, he combined them into a magnificent whole. His great strength lay in his handling of the English language, to which he brought a sweetness and lyricism that won immediate acceptance, his readings of very many passages surviving intact until they were enshrined in the Authorized Version. Indeed, Coverdale's version of the psalms was preferred by the divines who drew up the *Book of Common Prayer* in 1662 and it is his words which Anglican choirs still chant today.

To have produced the first complete translation of the Bible in English was one thing; to ensure its acceptance was another. For months van Meteren and his agents petitioned those in high places to seek the king's approval. James Nicholson, van Meteren's Southwark printer, sent specimen sections of the book to Master Secretary Cromwell in August 1535, together with a fulsome dedication to King Henry.

Coverdale and his backers clearly had a surer grasp of political reality than the zealous Tyndale. Their tactics brought swift results. Moreover, the timing was right; it was only a matter of weeks since Bishop John Fisher, Thomas More, and some Carthusian monks had been executed for denying the royal supremacy and Henry VIII was of a mind to undermine completely those who still supported papal authority. He had authorized preachers tour the country to denounce "the pretended authority of the bishops of Rome". An open Bible would be yet another useful weapon in his propaganda armoury; the people would be able to see for themselves the falseness of the papal claims. Henry scarcely needed the encouragement of Cromwell and Anne Boleyn to be favourably impressed by the Coverdale Bible. He ordered that copies should be sent to the bishops and some days later he summoned the leading ecclesiastics to Westminster to hear their verdict.

> *"Sire, the book has many faults,"* the conservative
> Gardiner ventured cautiously.

> *"But does it maintain any heresies?"* the king demanded.

> *"We have not been able to discover any actual heresies…"*

> *"If there be no heresies then, in God's name, let it go forth
> among our people."*

> *The interview was over.*[2]

Coverdale's translation was immediately successful. It was flying off the booksellers' shelves and, by the end of 1537, the original edition would be sold out and two reprints exhausted. Cromwell believed the time was propitious to move to the next stage of his religious programme, the establishment of an English Bible in every church by order. Everything was moving in favour of reform. The licensed preachers were doing their job well, despite the efforts of conservative bishops and clergy to hinder them. Confident of royal approval, Cromwell drew up a set of injunctions early in 1536. One of them ordered the parish clergy to set up a Bible in Latin and English in the choir of every church and to "comfort, exhort, and admonish every man to read the same as the very word of God and the spiritual food of man's soul".

Then, in May, occurred one of those political reverses which were not infrequent at the court of Henry VIII: Anne Boleyn, by a compound of her own folly and the machinations of her enemies, was brought to the Tower and thence to the block. This was not the prelude to a Catholic reaction but it served as a warning to Master Secretary. He quietly shelved the Bible injunction for the time being.

What had happened to Tyndale's Bible all this time? The task of completing it was taken up by one John Rogers, who had arrived in Antwerp in 1534 as chaplain to the English merchant community but had quickly fallen under Tyndale's spell. When Tyndale was arrested in the spring of 1535, he entrusted to Rogers the completion of his great task. Rogers moved to Wittenberg, to work on his translation in safety. What he produced was a mishmash. The New Testament and the Old Testament from Genesis to II Chronicles and Jonah was the work of Tyndale. The remainder of the book was taken from Coverdale's Bible. Rogers added over two thousand glosses, most of which were also culled from continental Protestants. These notes were less violent in tone than Tyndale's but they were still controversial, and Rogers was sufficiently dubious about the book's reception to put it out under a pseudonym. The title page bore the legend, "truly and purely translated into English by Thomas Matthew", and this version came to be known as Matthew's Bible.

Matthew's Bible was bankrolled by two astute London merchants, Richard Grafton and Edward Whitchurch. They risked their capital in the belief that the trend of royal policy had opened up a market big enough to sustain two vernacular Bibles. The partners had in mind a sumptuous, richly illustrated, luxury volume which would be bought by churches and wealthy bibliophiles. The printing was done in Antwerp because continental craftsmen were well ahead of their English counterparts in this kind of operation. No London printshop was equipped to tackle Grafton and Whitchurch's ambitious project. The first batch was imported into England in July 1537. Grafton immediately presented some copies to the archbishop of Canterbury. He passed it on to Cromwell and Cromwell gained the king's permission for the book to go on sale.

Coverdale and Rogers may have intended no rivalry to exist between their respective versions, but the same was not true of their backers. New, cheaper editions of the Coverdale Bible were produced by the printer, John Nicholson, and this caused Grafton to fear that his market might be undermined. He wrote to Cromwell, beseeching the minister to grant a monopoly to Matthew's Bible and to prevent its being pirated by unscrupulous rivals. But Cromwell refused to take sides, and for the time being the two English Bibles were left to compete for their share of the large and enthusiastic market.

Thus, by 1538, the English church was served by two vernacular Bibles, neither of which was above criticism. Coverdale's Bible was not a new translation from Greek and Hebrew originals; Matthew's Bible offended many because of its evangelical glosses. The promoters of free access to Scripture had been too successful! Variant readings gave rise to dissensions and there was a risk that rivalry would undermine the work of disseminating vernacular Scriptures. What was needed was an official, approved version which would win widespread acceptance.

The Great Bible

Cromwell's solution to the problem was characteristically simple and direct. He planned a new English Bible which would be achieved by setting the best and most amenable freelance translator available to revise the text acknowledged by scholars to be the best yet produced. The man was Coverdale; the book was Matthew's Bible, the most accurate translation available based largely on the original Greek and Hebrew. Thus, early in 1538, Miles Coverdale was set to revise John Rogers's book.

Speed was of the essence. Publication was entrusted to Grafton and Whitchurch because they had better resources, experience, and contacts than any of their rivals. Cromwell decided to print in Paris because "printing is finer there than elsewhere, and with the great number of printers and abundance of paper, books are dispatched sooner than in any other country".[3] Cromwell himself invested £400 in the venture. He was taking a huge risk. France was a Catholic country and the bishops had their spies everywhere.

For some months all went well and, in September 1538, Cromwell confidently issued his injunction that every parish was to acquire a copy of the new Bible before Easter 1539. But the French inquisitor-general became suspicious. In December the printshop was invaded. The completed sheets and the printing formes were confiscated and the workshop closed.

With time running short and the reformers' enemies on both sides of the Channel working together to hamper the project, what ensued was an exciting escapade reminiscent of the adventures of the Scarlet Pimpernel. Workmen and unconfiscated copies were smuggled out of France. The printers were installed in London premises. There, throughout March and early April, the Great Bible was completed. Even the phlegmatic Cromwell must have breathed a sigh of relief when he at last held in his hands a copy of the first authorized English Bible. The title page flatteringly but cunningly associated Henry VIII with the new book. The king was depicted handing Bibles to Cromwell and Cranmer, who in turn distributed them to a crowd of grateful people who called out *"vivat rex"* and "God Save the King".

Henry was never as enthusiastic about the English Bible as that picture suggests but his colours had now been firmly nailed to the mast for him and there could be no going back. Parish priests dutifully bought the book, as did many enthusiastic laymen. The first edition was soon exhausted and another appeared in April 1540, its price fixed by the government at ten shillings – very reasonable for what was a fine production. By the end of 1541 the Great Bible had gone through seven printings. Everyone concerned in the venture, whatever his motives, had good reason to be pleased. Everyone, that is, except Thomas Cromwell. In July 1540 the enemies of the king's chief minister had triumphed and brought him to his death on Tower Hill.

But no amount of intrigue could murder Cromwell's brainchild – the Great Bible. That Bible made such an impact on English society that Cranmer's words in a letter of 13 August 1537 to Cromwell can scarcely be regarded as exaggeration:

> *These shall be to give you the most hearty thanks that*
> *any heart can think, and that in the name of all of them*
> *which favoureth God's word, for your diligence at this time*
> *in procuring the king's highness to set forth God's word*
> *and his Gospel by his Grace's authority. For the which*
> *act, not only the king's majesty, but also you shall have a*
> *perpetual laud and memory of all them that be now, or*
> *hereafter shall be, God's faithful people and favourers of*
> *His word. And this deed you shall hear at the great day,*
> *when all things shall be opened and made manifest.*[4]

The campaign which ended triumphantly in the setting up of the Great Bible was a major success in the war of the English Bible but that war still continued. It was one thing to enact laws but another to enforce them, let alone persuade people of their validity. One priest in Kent told his people that, far from having the Great Bible in church, they would not see it until doomsday. When the people

of Wincanton, Somerset, approached their incumbent on the
matter, he denounced all "new-fangled fellows which read the new
books, for they be heretics and knaves and pharisees". They were,
he said, like "a dog that gnaweth a marrow bone and never cometh
to the pith". Richard Bush, priest of Hastings, went so far as to
wish to see the new translation burned.[5]

In many places the enemies of the Bible had no need to protect
people from it; they could rely on general apathy.

> *The most sacred and holy Bible is now had among us
> in our vulgar tongue, and freely permitted to be read of
> all men universally, at times convenient, without any
> let or perturbation, even in the churches: but how many
> read it? Verily a man may come into some churches and
> see the Bible so enclosed and wrapped about with dust,
> even as the pulpit in like manner is both with dust and
> cobwebs, that with his finger he may write upon the Bible
> this epitaph: ecce nunc in pulvere dormio, that is to say,
> "behold I sleep now in the dust". So little pleasure have
> these filthy swine and currish dogs in that most sweet and
> singular treasure.[6]*

So one reformer complained in 1541.

But it was not so everywhere. Up and down the country
the Great Bible produced a new breed of men and women
unlicensed "gospellers". They were literate people, though often
of no formal education, who espoused the new doctrines and
expounded them to whoever would listen from the public Bibles
in the churches. Often they chose to do this during mass, setting
up a "rival show" and sometimes drowning the mumblings of the
priest in the sanctuary. A local layman, William Maldon, related
how the poor men of Chelmsford came together on Sundays "in
the lower end of the church... to hear their reading of that glad
and sweet tidings of the Gospel".[7] Bishop Bonner of London set
up a placard over the Bible in St Paul's urging people to read
quietly to themselves, not to draw crowds together or attempt

unlicensed exposition and particularly not to read aloud during divine service.

In the face of pressure from conservatives Henry got cold feet. In 1542 printing was halted and no more copies were published under royal licence during Henry's reign. Another blow came the following year when Parliament passed the Act for the Advancement of True Religion and for the Abolishment of the Contrary. This measure completely outlawed Tyndale's translations and stated that other English versions of Scripture might only be kept if all "annotations and preambles" were excised. Unlicensed persons were forbidden to read aloud from the Bible in church. The statute announced that many of "the lower sort" had abused the privilege of the open Bible. Therefore, on pain of one month's imprisonment, "no women, nor artificers, prentices, journeymen, servingmen of the degrees of yeomen or under, husbandmen nor labourers shall read the Bible or New Testament in English to himself or any other, privately or openly".[8]

The advocates of an open Bible had always hoped that it would change society. The enemies of an open Bible had always feared that it would change society. Those hopes and fears were now being realized but not in way that anyone had expected.

As the pain-racked life of the obese, irascible Henry VIII drew to its close, English religion was in a state of confusion. In some churches groups of evangelicals were meeting for Bible study, gathered around the precious chained volume. In others the Great Bible was tucked away in an inaccessible corner or not available at all. Members of the English church were opting, as they have ever since, for either a priest-dominated or a Bible-based religion. The king, genuinely dismayed by the situation, was powerless to change it. On Christmas Eve 1545 he hobbled into the Parliament house and delivered a moving speech in which he deplored

> *how unreverently that most precious jewel, the word of God, is disputed, rhymed, sung and jangled in every alehouse and tavern, contrary to the true meaning and doctrine of the same.*

Seven months later he issued a proclamation:

> *From henceforth no man, woman or person of what*
> *estate condition or degree soever he or they be... shall*
> *have, take or keep in his or their possession the text of the*
> *New Testament of Tyndale's or Coverdale's translation*
> *in English, nor any other than is permitted by the Act*
> *of Parliament made in the session of parliament held at*
> *Westminster in the four and thirtieth and five and thirtieth*
> *year of his Majesty's most noble reign; nor... any manner*
> *of books printed or written in the English tongue which*
> *he or shall be set forth in the names of Frith, Tyndale,*
> *Wycliffe, Joye, Roy, Basil, Bale, Barnes, Coverdale,*
> *Turner, Tracy...*[9]

Banned books were to be handed in by 1 October for burning. The Catholic pyromaniacs had a field day, many believing or pretending to believe that the proclamation involved all English Bibles, including those printed under royal licence.

Reformation and Reaction 1547–58

Everything changed when Henry VIII's nine-year-old son came to the throne as Edward VI. The old king had tried to balance England's religious parties but his son had been brought up by committed evangelicals and it was his radical mentors – Edward Seymour, duke of Somerset (1547–49) and John Dudley, duke of Northumberland (1550–53) – who governed in his name. For the twelve years following Henry's death, when Edward VI and later his Catholic sister, Mary I, ruled, conviction politics held sway.

One of the first measures taken by Seymour's government was the removal of all restrictions on the printing, publication, and reading of English Bibles. In July a fresh injunction went out concerning the purchase of the Great Bible by churches.

Every parish was given three months to equip itself with "the whole Bible of the largest volume in English".

Now that vernacular Scriptures could be bought openly, there was considerable demand for the various versions available. Tyndale's works, for instance, went through seventeen editions during the brief reign of the boy-king.

Thomas Cranmer was still archbishop of Canterbury and now he enjoyed the freedom to complete the reform of the English church, providing it with a new vernacular liturgy and ensuring that the Scriptures were at the heart of its life. The first move Cranmer made was to have the English Bible read aloud during services. As early as 1543 parish priests had been required to read one chapter of Scripture every Sunday between the *Te Deum* and the *Magnificat* but this instruction had been honoured more in the breach than in the observance. Now (1547) a new injunction ordered that the epistle and Gospel at high mass were to be read in English. Furthermore, there was to be a visitation of all churches to ensure, among other things, that this regulation was complied with. At the same time Cranmer began to establish the doctrinal basis of the new regime. He published a book of twelve homilies or sermons, with instructions that they were to be read to congregations by clergy who could not or would not preach. The homilies covered many aspects of faith and morals, but the first was on the authority and use of Scripture. The author stressed that Scripture was the only ground of our faith. All men should seek to study the word of God and not be content only to hear it read. The homily was not only simple and direct in its language; it was also written in beautiful prose: "The Scripture is full, as well of low valleys, plain ways, and easy for every man to use and to walk in, as also of high hills and mountains, which few men can ascend unto."[10]

But the principal task to which Cranmer addressed himself now, and the one for which he will always be remembered, was the *Book of Common Prayer*. In January 1549 Parliament passed an Act of Uniformity that introduced Cranmer's new prayer book and ordained that its universal use was to commence on Whit Sunday (9 June). By the same date all old service books were to be handed in for burning.

From the beginning the Prayer Book and the Bible were thought of as two sides of the coin of English church life. All the old missals, breviaries, psalters, and other service books were to be swept away; henceforth the clergy only needed the two vernacular books to lead their people in worship. And the Prayer Book was itself saturated in Scripture. The preface to the new book clearly stated that nothing was to be read in the services "but the very pure word of God, the holy Scriptures, or that which is evidently grounded upon the same".

The new book contained a monthly table for the recitation of the psalms and a calendar detailing the readings of Old and New Testament lessons at matins and evensong. In order to facilitate the conduct of public worship, the Psalter from the Great Bible was published separately in 1549. It replaced other versions of the psalms then in use and became the only official translation to be used. Coverdale's musical cadences have never been improved upon and many of his linguistic gems have become the common heritage of people of all shades of religious opinion. Many would recognize such words as:

> *Yea, though I walk through the valley of the shadow of death, I will fear no evil: for thou art with me; thy rod and thy staff comfort me. [Psalm 23:4]*

> *God is our hope and strength: a very present help in trouble. [Psalm 46:1]*

> *O come, let us worship and fall down: and kneel before the Lord our maker. [Psalm 95:6]*

And, of course, the same is supremely true of the Lord's Prayer. No other version of Jesus' pattern prayer, though couched in modern language, though more easily understandable, has ever replaced Coverdale's rendering for most English-speaking people.

Then, in 1553, everything changed once again. Edward VI died and the zealously Catholic Mary Tudor came to the throne. She was determined to undo as much as possible of her father's and half-brother's Reformation. There is no doubt that the new regime would have removed the English Bible from the face of the earth if it could have done so. The queen's attitude was made graphically clear one day in 1554 as she rode through London with her husband, Philip II of Spain. In Gracechurch Street she saw a painted picture which showed Henry VIII delivering to his son Edward a book bearing the legend *Verbum Dei*. Presumably it had been erected by London Protestants as a broad hint that any action taken against the English Bible would be treason to the memory of her father and her half-brother. The jibe did not fail of its desired effect. Mary was furious and she told Stephen Gardiner, the conservative Bishop of Winchester and now also lord chancellor, to seek out the people responsible. Gardiner tracked down the painter and berated him as villain, knave, and traitor. He made the man erase the book and the offensive words.

But Mary made no attempt to outlaw the English Bible. Why this reluctance to strike at the very heart of Protestantism, the source of all heresies? It would have been easy enough to have the Great Bible removed from the churches; many parishes, as we shall see, had of their own volition taken the book away. Book bonfires had once more become familiar sights. Why could not the vernacular Scriptures be consigned to the flames? The answer is that, for all that Mary favoured the calling in of the Great Bible, her advisers – men like Gardiner and Bonner – realized that such a step would be provocative and ineffective. They had been carrying out purges of heretical literature for a quarter of a century and they knew that the results were seldom satisfactory. Books could be easily hidden or smuggled away and for every one burned there were always scores that were never found. They remembered also the furore which had followed the restrictions on Bible reading in 1543. Then, the forbidding of the Great Bible to simple people had roused a storm of protest. During the dozen or so years that had passed since then, countless numbers of English men and women had come to love the Bible. A fresh move to bar it would have dashed any slender hope Mary may have had of winning the hearts of her subjects.

If the English Bible came under no official attack, it suffered considerably at the hands of Catholic zealots. At Frodsham, Cheshire, "all the books of the church were delivered to the dean, and were by him burned at Budworth". Three villages in Durham reported: "… all their books that they had in King Edward's time were delivered to the chancellor and were burned." "The Bible, the communion book and other books were burned" at Hawton near Newark.[11] It was the same all over the country; conservative officials could scarcely wait to get rid of the offending books. As soon as they saw the trend of the new administration, they took the law into their own hands. Not all the Great Bibles disappeared. Where the book was revered, it remained unmolested in its accustomed place or was taken away and hidden. It was the story of religious images over again. Everything depended on the sentiment and beliefs of the local priest and people. When the brief reign of "Bloody Mary" was over and churches were ordered once again to display copies of the Great Bible, there were many parishes which had no need to go to the expense of acquiring a new copy; they still had the books they had bought during the reign of Henry or Edward.

Far worse than the unauthorized assaults on Protestant literature was the persecution unleashed by the government of men and women who refused to renounce their evangelical faith. During Mary's reign, England had a taste of the Spanish Inquisition. Almost 300 people were burned at the stake. In addition, countless others were imprisoned and either died under torture or were forced to recant. But the next chapter of the story of the English Bible was written by a third group.

The Geneva Bible

Within months of Mary's rapturous welcome in London, Protestant exiles had begun to leave England. The majority of them came from the influential classes – men and women of wealth who could afford to leave family and lands, educated men and women who actually looked forward to meeting their continental co-religionists who were teaching and preaching in the leading centres of European reform. Most settled at Strasbourg, Wesel, Emden, Zürich, Basel, Aarau, Frankfurt, and Geneva. It is to the English communities at these last two named towns that we must now turn our attention. Among the 200 or so exiles that took up residence in the free imperial city of Frankfurt-am-Main in the summer of 1554 was a thirty-year-old Oxford graduate called William Whittingham. He was a good scholar, had already travelled widely on the continent, and was fluent in French and German. He also belonged to that extreme wing of the English church which later would be called the Puritans. In other words he adhered to the doctrines formulated by John Calvin, the leader of the Genevan church, from which several other congregations drew their allegiance. Briefly the main points of Calvin's teaching (which were not necessarily accepted by all Protestants) were as follows: By his sovereign and irresistible will God predestines the "elect" to salvation and the rest of mankind to damnation. A person receives his election when the Holy Spirit in his heart enables him to respond to the word of salvation contained in Scripture. The same Spirit draws the believer to progressive holiness and this is an outward manifestation of his election. Just as the individual should aim for purity and simplicity of life, so should these be the marks of the church. All later excrescences must be purged away from the organization and worship of the church, which must follow the simple patterns of the New Testament congregations.

In September 1555 Whittingham moved on to Geneva. He found the atmosphere of the godly commonwealth as invigorating and uplifting as the Alpine air. He became an elder and subsequently a minister in the English church, which was organized on Calvinist principles and, according to tradition, he married a sister or sister-in-law of the great reformer.

Now Whittingham and his colleagues could settle to the task of planning the purification of religion in their homeland, and first they addressed themselves to producing a new translation of the Bible. The place and time could scarcely have been better chosen. Geneva, as Whittingham said, was a "store of heavenly learning and judgement". Calvin himself was an excellent biblical scholar and writer of commentaries, and the town also contained Theodore Beza, probably the greatest living expert on the Greek and Hebrew texts. Also in Geneva for the best part of a year (1558–59) was the aged and experienced translator, Miles Coverdale. With such men to advise him Whittingham at first set to work on the New Testament, taking Tyndale's work as his basis and revising it in accordance with the Greek. He added copious notes to explain the text: "I have [explained] all such places by the best learned interpreters as either were falsely expounded by some or else absurdly applied by others: so that by this means both they which have not ability to buy the commentaries upon the New Testament, and they also which have not opportunity and leisure to read them because of their prolixity may use this book in stead thereof."[12] The most important contribution which this book made to the progress of the English Bible was the division of the text into verses, a device which has been used ever since.

The New Testament was published in 1557 but Whittingham and his friends were still hard at work. All the time that could be spared from preaching and pastoral work was devoted to the arduous labour of translation. Two versions of the Psalms appeared in 1557 and 1559. But all the previous work was subsumed into the great Geneva Bible of 1560. This version, sometimes known as the Breeches Bible because of its rendering of Genesis 3:7, "And they sewed fig leaves together, and made themselves breeches", was one of the major milestones in the history of the English Scriptures. First of all it was a most scrupulous piece of translation, basically being a revision of the Great Bible and of Tyndale's fragments. The translators took their time, consulted the best scholars available, and used the best original texts. Where there were possible variant readings to the ones chosen, they were noted in the margin. Words which had been added in the English to help the flow of the text were printed in italics and the verse divisions were now applied throughout. The Geneva Bible contained many excellent turns of phrase which were to survive unchanged in the King James Version. For example, such memorable passages as I Corinthians 13:12 scarcely needed any alteration in 1611, the Genevan translators having given us such gems as "For now we see through a glass darkly."

The preface, chapter headings, and marginal notes in the Geneva Bible ran to over 300,000 words and included maps and other "scientific" information about the Holy Land. The notes made the book the most effective piece of propaganda the Calvinist party ever produced. The reader was carefully directed as to how he or she should understand the text, especially those passages which had a bearing on current theological issues. Thus for the book of Revelation the translators provided notes (which were often longer than the passages they were illuminating) which clearly identified the Antichrist with the Church of Rome and urged all Christians to root out without mercy every vestige of popery.

Long before the Geneva Bible was finished, English political and religious life had lurched in another direction. In November 1558 Mary died to be replaced by her younger half-sister, Elizabeth. She was a cautious friend of reform and the exiles hurried home to take their place in the English Protestant church, determined to push it in a more extreme direction. However, Whittingham and his friends stayed on to see their great work completed. The complete new Bible finally made its appearance on 10 April 1560.

The work was dedicated to Queen Elizabeth, and its creators did not hesitate to point out Her Majesty's duty in the dedicatory epistle:

> *The eyes of all that fear God in all places behold your*
> *countries as an example to all that believe, and the*
> *prayers of all the godly at all times are directed to God*
> *for the preservation of your Majesty. For considering*
> *God's wonderful mercies towards you at all seasons, who*
> *hath pulled you out of the mouth of the lions, and how*
> *that from your youth you have been brought up in the*
> *holy Scriptures, the hope of all men is so increased, that*
> *they cannot but look that God should bring to pass some*
> *wonderful work by your Grace to the universal comfort of*
> *his church. Therefore even above strength you must show*

yourself strong and bold in God's matters… This Lord
of lords and King of kings who hath ever defended his,
strengthen, comfort and preserve your Majesty, that you
may be able to build up the ruins of God's house to his
glory, the discharge of your conscience, and to the comfort
of all them that love the coming of Christ Jesus our Lord.

When the promoters of the Geneva Bible arrived home, they encountered a situation which, on the face of it, could not have been more favourable. The queen had issued an injunction which had a familiar ring: every church was "to provide within three months after this visitation, at the charges of the parish, one book of the whole Bible of the largest volume in English".

There was, apparently, nothing to prevent the Geneva Bible going on sale alongside the Great Bible. Elizabeth granted a seven-year printing monopoly to the Devon-born John Bodley, one of the returning exiles. However the royal licence had a sting in its tail. The book might only be printed in England,

provided that the Bible to be imprinted may be so ordered
in the edition thereof as may… seem expedient by the
advice of our trusty and wellbeloved the bishops of
Canterbury and London.[13]

Archbishop Matthew Parker, who had spent Mary's reign in hiding rather than go into exile, was, like many of the ecclesiastical top brass, wary of a takeover by the Calvinist party, which was beginning to be known as "Puritan". Bodley, with one eye to the considerable outlay he had made, might have been prepared to consider some amendments to satisfy the bishops. What is quite certain is that Whittingham and his colleagues were not prepared to submit their translation for episcopal approval. So Bodley's Bible continued to be printed in Geneva and to be freely imported into England.

If the Devonian merchant was worried about the financial success of the venture, reassurance came speedily. The Geneva

Bible was bought eagerly by returned exiles, by their families and friends, and by many others who had no connection with what now emerged as the "Puritan" party. The reformed Elizabethan church was Calvinist in its theology but less so in its liturgy. Puritans were those who wanted Reformation to be carried to its logical conclusion by, for example, the banning of religious images and vestments. Its success was immediate and it became the bestseller of the Elizabethan age. During the Queen's reign alone it went through forty impressions, and for at least two generations thereafter it was to be the most popular Bible for family reading and private devotional use. But, despite frequent petitions, Bodley could not obtain permission to print in England.

The Bishops' Bible

The basic problem was the one that had been around for half a century. The men with the ability and motivation to produce English Bibles were partisan reformers who could scarcely avoid using the text as a vehicle for carrying their own convictions, while the establishment men who wanted to free Scripture from radical interpretation lacked the zeal and, in most cases, the scholarship to carry out the necessary work.

However, Parker was determined to reduce Puritan influence. It was by now obvious that the Geneva Bible could only be outfaced by a version of the Great Bible purged of all scholarly defects and made as accurate as was humanly possible. In 1561 he set about producing just such a version. What came to be known as the Bishops' Bible was not completed until 1568. It was the work of a committee. Parker divided the Bible up into sections , which were distributed to thirteen leading scholars, most of them bishops. Other experts were called upon to give guidance and make corrections. Parker, who retained overall responsibility, gave explicit instructions to his team. They were to follow the Great Bible carefully and only correct it in the interests of greater faithfulness to the original Hebrew and Greek. They were "to make no bitter notes upon any text or yet to set down any determination in places of controversy". Passages such as long genealogies which were less edifying than others should be marked so that they could be avoided in public reading. These requirements were all admirable. Unfortunately, however, Parker then introduced a note of prudery: "… such words as soundeth in the old translation to any offence or lightness or obscenity" were to be "expressed with more convenient terms and phrases".[14] Inevitably some contributors took longer than others and some were more conscientious. Patiently Parker cajoled and chivvied his colleagues, checking and rechecking their work. At last, on 5 October 1568, the archbishop was able to send a copy of the new book to the queen.

The result of all this patient labour was, perhaps inevitably, a disappointment. The Bishops' Bible, though unsurpassed for accuracy, was rendered in stiff, cold English. It lacked the fluidity, the warmth of the version which the close-knit group of exiles had infused into the Geneva Bible. Convocation, the church's parliament, ordered that all the bishops should buy a copy, that one must be set up in each cathedral, and that parish churches should obtain copies "as far as can conveniently be done". Parker asked the queen to sanction the Bishops' Bible as the only one permitted for use in public worship and to grant a monopoly to the printer, Richard Jugge. Neither petition was granted. The Bishops' Bible was not to be the main religious and literary influence on the age of Shakespeare. That privilege was reserved for the Geneva Bible. Most of the sixteenth-century Bibles and testaments were now freely circulating in England but the book produced by the exiles retained pride of place in the affection of the people.

What had clearly emerged by this time was that those who supported Bible reading did so for a variety of reasons. If we leave aside purely commercial considerations – the profit motive – we can identify at least three kinds of aficionados. Some were spurred on by the evangelical impulse. They drove home the message of Scripture by glosses and marginalia. Then there were the scholars, still intent on providing as accurate a translation as possible. Thirdly there were the establishment men, the leaders of church and state. They wanted a "safe" Bible; one that would help unite the nation behind the ecclesiastical status quo. Interaction between these interest groups would shape the King James Version.

The Douai-Rheims Bible

But there was yet one more English Bible produced in the sixteenth century. Like Tyndale's books this one was born in the Low Countries. Douai lies less than 150 kilometres to the north-east of Antwerp. It was here that William Allen, a Jesuit biblical scholar of considerable repute, had established an English College for the purpose of training young Englishmen to be Catholic missionaries in their own land. Reactionary in his intentions, Allen knew the importance of being radical in his methods. He decided to take a leaf out of the enemy's book. The Protestants had made the English Bible the focus of their appeal to the people. Very well, the students of Douai must be equally well versed in Scripture.

> *Since it is of great consequence that they should be familiar with the text of holy Scripture and its more approved meanings, and have at their finger ends all those passages which are correctly used by Catholics in support of our faith, or impiously misused by heretics in opposition to the church's faith, we provide for them, as a means by which they may gain this power, a daily lecture in the New Testament in which the exact and genuine sense of the words is briefly dictated to them. Every day at table after dinner and supper, before they leave their places, they hear a running explanation of one chapter of the Old and another of the New Testament. At suitable times they take down from dictation, with references to the controversies of the present day, all those passages of holy Scripture, which either make for Catholics or are distorted by heretics, together with short notes concerning the argument to be drawn from the one and the answers to be made to the other.* [15]

The trainee missionaries at Douai, and later at Rheims, whither
the college moved in 1578, studied the entire Old Testament twelve
times and the New Testament sixteen times during the three-year
course. But Allen was still not satisfied.

> *Our adversaries... have at their fingers' ends from*
> *some heretical version, all those passages of Scripture*
> *which seem to make for them, and by a certain deceptive*
> *adaptation and alteration of the sacred words produce the*
> *effect of appearing to say nothing but what comes from*
> *the Bible. This evil might be remedied if we too had some*
> *Catholic version of the Bible.[16]*

It was the final accolade. Did Wycliffe and Tyndale smile at each
other in heaven? The importance of the vernacular Scriptures,
which they had maintained against violent Catholic opposition,
was now acknowledged by the enemy.

Allen's challenge was taken up by Gregory Martin, a scholar
who had been a chaplain and tutor to the Catholic Howard family
before going to the English College as lecturer in Hebrew and the
Bible. Martin started with the New Testament, basing his translation
on the Vulgate but referring closely to the Greek. The book was
published at Rheims in 1582. It was a polemical work set forth for
quite different reasons than all the other English translations. The
preface made this quite clear:

> *We do not publish upon erroneous opinion of necessity,*
> *that the holy Scriptures should always be in our mother*
> *tongue, or that they ought, or were ordained by God, to be*
> *read indifferently of all ... but upon special consideration*
> *of the present time, state and condition of our country,*
> *unto which divers things are either necessary, or profitable*
> *and medicinal now, that otherwise in the peace of the*
> *church were neither much requisite, nor perchance wholly*
> *tolerable.*

Nothing could more clearly express the difference between Protestant and Catholic attitudes towards the Bible. There is no "heretical nonsense" here about the necessity of free access to the life-giving word of God. The marginal notes of the Rheims Testament were tendentious in the extreme, urging Catholic doctrines, challenging Protestant interpretations of Scripture and attacking "the false and vain glosses of Calvin and his followers". The text itself suffered from too great a devotion to the Vulgate. Latinisms abounded and in some places obscured the meaning. The translator's main objective was to make the text support existing Catholic doctrine and practice, introducing – inaccurately – words such as "host", "chalice", and "penance". The Catholics at Rheims continued their work on the Old Testament in the same vein. They completed their Bible in 1609–10. By then another English version destined to outlive all rivals was nearing completion – the King James Version.

CHAPTER 4

NO END OF
TRANSLATING

In 1603, when James VI of Scotland ascended the English throne as James I, Bible translation had passed through two dramatic and, at times, bloody centuries. Its impact had been profound. The educational standards of the clergy had improved noticeably. More of them possessed, and presumably used in instructing their flocks, Bibles and other books. The emphasis in clerical libraries had moved away from the medieval collections of wondrous tales of saintly miracles to works by the Church fathers and contemporary reformist theologians. In some parts of the country Puritans organized regular "exercises", gatherings of the local clergy to hear expositions of Scripture and to study the Bible together. Vicars and rectors were under pressure to make themselves familiar with the word of God. They were expected to preach regularly and their pulpit performances were likely to be compared with those of neighbouring colleagues. More of them were now faced in the pews by literate parishioners who were devout Bible students and might challenge the interpretation of their chosen texts.

Surviving notebooks give us an indication of how some clergy prepared their sermons. Robert Dobbs, vicar of Runcorn from 1580 to 1621, expounded the doctrine of predestination and listed the Scripture references that supported it. He made lists of sermon topics such as the eight benefits of the passion of Christ and the five ways in which Christians experience divine guidance.[1]

Such exemplars were, admittedly, rare and bishops' visitations did still continue to lament the overall standard of clerical competence, but things were improving. Sermons, however, were not the only media for conveying Scripture to congregations. As we have seen, readings from the English Bible were designated for every service and the Prayer Book itself was steeped in biblical language. The recitation of psalms and canticles infiltrated the language of Scripture into people's minds. Phrases such as "Lord now lettest thou thy servant depart in peace", "The Lord is my shepherd" and "The fear of the Lord is the beginning of wisdom" became verbal commonplaces.

In many places worshippers only had to look around them to become aware that word had replaced image in the decoration of churches. Once polychromed pictures of St Christopher, St Michael, the Virgin Mary, and the Last Judgment had filled internal wall spaces. These had now been whitewashed over and replaced by the Ten Commandments, the Lord's Prayer, and a variety of Scripture texts. Elizabeth had been particularly concerned about the barrenness of church interiors. Early in her reign she had ordered that wooden panels with the Commandments painted on them

> be comely set, or hung up in the east end of the chancel,
> to be not only read for edification, but also to give some
> comely ornament and demonstration, that the same is a
> place of religion and prayer.[2]

There were, thus, many ways in which the Bible was entering the stream of consciousness of the English people. For those who studied it personally there were now no fewer than six versions of vernacular Scripture available (though those bearing the names of Matthew, Coverdale, and the Great Bible, had passed out of print). Small wonder that, when a new translating initiative was mooted, Bishop Bancroft of London retorted, "If every man's humour should be followed there would be no end of translating."[3] Most people were in sympathy with Bancroft. Every section of the church in England had its favourite version. Puritans had the Geneva Bible with its radical glosses. Those who wanted an unadorned text had the Bishops' Bible. Catholic recusants and their priests could read the partisan Douai-Rheims Bible. On the face of it English society could manage perfectly well without seeking the Holy Grail of a more perfect volume of vernacular Scripture. But there were tensions below the surface of English religious and political life and these came to the surface with the arrival of a new monarch. It was this which, quite unexpectedly, led to the creation of the King James Version.

It has sometimes been said that Elizabeth I's church had a Calvinist theology and a Catholic liturgy. For most of the queen's reign she and her ministers had been in conflict with the Catholic powers of Spain and France; these were backed by the pope, who had excommunicated the queen and was encouraging infiltrators from William Allen's college to stir up rebellion. This and, particularly, the invasion threat posed by the Spanish Armada encouraged nationalist fervour in England and strengthened the hands of the Puritans. Many of Elizabeth's ministers and councillors were men who had learned their theology as members of Calvinist congregations in exile. The queen herself, however, was no lover of the liturgical austerities the Puritans wished to impose. She enjoyed colour, ceremony, and ritual and set her face against iconoclasm. Towards the end of the reign, as the old Marian exiles died, she advanced men of moderate views. Men like Lancelot Andrewes (royal chaplain and dean of Westminster), John Whitgift (archbishop of Canterbury from 1583), and Richard Hooker (author of the *Laws of Ecclesiastical Polity*) were a new breed

– "Anglicans" – who believed in the triple authority of Scripture, Church, and Reason. They thought that the Church of England had reached a state of near perfection and opposed Puritans who claimed to find in the Bible justification for demanding further reform of liturgy and ecclesiastical order. Whitgift insisted,

> *I find no one, certain and perfect kind of government prescribed or commanded in the Scriptures to the church of Christ; which no doubt should have been done, if it had been a matter necessary unto salvation of the church. Secondly, because the essential notes of the church be these only: the true preaching of the word of God, and the right administration of the sacraments… so that, notwithstanding government, or some kind of government, may be a part of the church, touching the outward form and perfection of it, yet is not such a part of the essence and being, but that it may be the church of Christ without this or that kind of government, and therefore the "kind of government" of the church is not "necessary unto salvation".*[4]

Moreover, Whitgift solemnly warned Puritan objectors to examine their motives carefully:

> *I do charge all men before God and his angels as they will answer at the day of judgement, that under the pretext of zeal they seek not to spoil the church; under the colour of perfection they work not confusion; under the cloak of simplicity they cover not pride, ambition, vainglory, arrogance; under the outward show of godliness they nourish not contempt of magistrates, popularity, anabaptistry, and sundry other pernicious and pestilent errors.*[5]

On episcopacy Richard Hooker was quite adamant:

A thousand five hundred years and upward the church of
Christ hath now continued under the sacred regiment of
bishops. Neither for so long hath Christianity been ever
planted in any kingdom throughout the world but with this
kind of government alone; which to have been ordained of
God, I am for mine own part even as resolutely persuaded,
as that any other kind of government in the world
whatsoever is of God.[6]

Although the English church had disembarrassed itself of Roman dogma, papal obedience, and most of the outward trappings of continental Catholicism, the fundamental question still remained, in the view of some, unresolved: was ultimate authority vested in the Bible or the episcopal hierarchy? Whitgift imposed severe restrictions on preachers and on the press, and strengthened the church courts to deal with all dissidents. This policy had its culmination in the Canons of 1604, which excommunicated all who spoke against the accepted governmental and liturgical forms of the church, such as those who "shall hereafter affirm, that the government of the Church of England under His Majesty by archbishops, bishops, deans, archdeacons, and the rest that bear office in the same, is antichristian or repugnant to the world of God".

The methods of Whitgift and his colleagues were largely successful. The government could not stamp out private gatherings for the celebration of unauthorized services or "prophesying", or stop the faithful flocking to hear radical preachers. It could and did enforce an outwards conformity on the majority of parish clergy. The only men who stubbornly refused to be forced into the Anglican mould were the "Presbyterians" – extremist Puritans who believed that episcopacy was incompatible with the biblical revelation. They resigned their benefices rather than compromise with the "dregs of popery". However, discontent persisted among those who remained in office. They looked at bishops who lived in palaces enjoying the lifestyle of secular aristocrats and contrasted them with the elders who held sway in the first-century church.

Such critics continued to look for change. By the time of Elizabeth's death, Puritanism had lost none of its spiritual or moral strength but its influence throughout the country was very patchy.

The nation had changed dramatically long before 1603. England had become Europe's leading Protestant nation, an identity it had acquired in spite of, rather than because of, the queen's framing of policy. Elizabeth had been excommunicated by the pope, who exhorted loyal Catholics to bring about her overthrow. There had been plots and assassination attempts as well as frustrated invasions. The "victory" over Philip II's armada was celebrated annually after 1588. England had become the main haven for Huguenots and other European Protestants fleeing persecution. Threats to national security had helped to shape a new English identity. Probably few Englishmen thought of themselves as aggressively Protestant but the vast majority knew that they were anti-Catholic. England had "settled" into a comfortable, self-assured religious life. Parish churches had lost their "Catholic clutter" and the over-ornateness of medieval ritual and, if only a few had gone to the extreme of Genevan simplicity, most had adopted a chaste, conservative, reserved decor. Worshippers had grown accustomed to hearing (and sometimes even listening to!) sermons and could recite canticles and the creed.

The Arrival of James I

But the term "Elizabethan settlement" implies more than just the emergence of identifiable Anglican patterns of liturgy and decor. Religious fervour had abated. Two generations had passed since the heady, revivalist days of the 1530s and the Church of England was now the respectable spiritual home for the majority of Elizabeth's subjects. Reformation doctrine was no longer an exciting novelty and most people, after decades of turmoil, wanted a quiet life. Few religious radicals went to the stake for their beliefs and the last to be burned perished in 1593 (the last radical martyr was Edward Wightman, who was executed in 1611). Puritans were the zealots of the English church, ever campaigning for stricter morals, simpler worship, and a rigid adherence to Calvinist theology. But they were no longer the political force they had once been. Such former Puritan champions as William Cecil, Francis Walsingham, and Robert Dudley were dead and Elizabeth was very sensitive to the criticisms of "left wing" Protestants. She had effectively sacked the avowedly Puritan archbishop of Canterbury, Edmund Grindal (by refusing to allow him to carry out his official duties), and backed the efforts of his successor, John Whitgift, to curb Puritan excesses. Extremists could still make nuisances of themselves, as when an anonymous group printed the "Marprelate Tracts" in 1589–90 denouncing episcopacy, but the vigilance of the bishops kept the party in check and they were aided by popular disfavour. When Shakespeare lampooned Puritans as canting hypocrites in the person of Malvolio (*Twelfth Night*), he was undoubtedly taking advantage of common prejudice.

As far as the Bible was concerned, it no longer enjoyed the glamour of being a controversial book. Long gone were the days when copies had to be hidden and readers went in fear of the knock on the door in the dead of night. Anyone could now read the Bible and many did so. Many more did not. Most English men and women were only too happy that the decades of bitter religious rivalry were over, the more so when they heard stories of atrocities committed in the wars of religion raging in continental Europe. Certainly, there was no popular demand for another translation of the Bible. The government had tried to commend the *Bishops' Bible* to loyal subjects by commissioning a leading German engraver, Francis Hogenberg, to design a portrait frontispiece of the queen above the legend, "Let me not be ashamed to be an evangelist of Christ, for the strength of God is security for all believers." Such stratagems failed. Most people who read the Bible were not wooed away from the Geneva version.

The king who travelled from Edinburgh to London in the summer of 1603 was thirty-seven years of age and of very unprepossessing appearance. One foreign observer called him "an old young man". James was slightly under average height, his pale complexion emphasized by his red hair and beard. But it was his ungainly movements that made the biggest initial impression on those who met him for the first time. He had an awkward gait and was constantly fidgeting. He was boorish, particularly in female company, and there was nothing remotely dignified or regal about him. His nervous and introverted disposition can largely be put down to his upbringing. He had been crowned when he was one year old, by which time his father, Lord Darnley, had been murdered and his mother, Mary Queen of Scots, forced into exile in England, where she remained a prisoner of Queen Elizabeth until her execution in 1587. James was brought up by tutors chosen for him by noble factions and leaders of the Scottish (Presbyterian) Kirk. He had had to fight and scheme to assert his own authority.

James's greatest asset was a keen mind. Like many lonely children, he turned to books for companionship and proved himself a ready learner. Before he reached his teenage years he had mastered French, Latin, Greek, and Hebrew. Finding human communication difficult, he expressed himself in writing and produced mini-treatises on subjects as diverse as the art of kingship, the evils of tobacco, and the book of Revelation. James had a very exalted (though not entirely unmerited) opinion of his own intellectual ability. He considered himself something of a theologian and he certainly knew his Bible. He arrived in England as a man with a mission. He would impress upon the people that he was God's representative, come as a peacemaker to heal the divisions in the church.

Puritan leaders greeted with enthusiasm the prospect of a king who had been brought up by Presbyterians. They took the initiative very quickly. Scarcely had James set out from Edinburgh in April 1603 when he was met by a delegation of English Puritans who presented him with a Millenary Petition supposedly signed by 1,000 clergy. This document of requests urged the king to undertake to complete the English Reformation. "God, we trust, has appointed your Highness our physician" to heal the diseases of the church, they asserted, "and we say with Mordecai to Esther, 'who knoweth whether you are come to the kingdom for such a time?' " They asked the king to summon a conference at which all the abuses in the religious life of the nation could be discussed.

So, on the face of it, James and his new radical Protestant subjects had the same objective – the creation of an English church united in doctrine and worship. The reality, of course, was that there could be no agreement on what constituted true doctrine and worship. The objective of the new king was identical to that of the old queen – the subjection of church and state to God's anointed deputy. It was James's misfortune that he lacked Elizabeth's political weapons – a whole armoury of feminine wiles and smiles, cushioned threats, and gracious promises, well-rehearsed "impromptu" speeches, and assurances of love. James had not the slightest intention of weakening the rule of king and bishops and was bitterly opposed to anything that smacked of Scottish Presbytery. As a child he had fully accepted the doctrine and church polity of his mentors but with the passing of the years he had come to resent the hectoring of ministers and their assertions that the Scottish church was independent of the crown. The fiery preacher, James Melville, had told James to his face, "There are two kings and two kingdoms in Scotland. There is Christ Jesus the king and his kingdom the kirk, whose subject King James is." In this kingdom James Stuart was merely one member among many. He adopted a clean contrary viewpoint. In a treatise, *Basilicon Doron*, written to tutor his son in the theory and practice of kingship, he wrote, "Ye have a double obligation; first for that [God] made you a man; and next for that he made you a little God to sit on his throne and rule over other men."[7] The king, he asserted, was God's appointed deputy, supreme in both state *and* church. By this time (1599) he had developed an almost pathological hatred of Melville and his ilk. They were, he thundered,

> *Very pests in the church and commonwealth: whom*
> *no desserts can oblige, neither oaths or promises bind;*
> *breathing nothing but sedition and calumnies, aspiring*
> *without measure, railing without reason, and making their*
> *own imaginations (without any warrant of the world)*

the square of their conscience. I protest before the great
God… that ye shall never find with any Highland or
Border thieves greater ingratitude and more lies and vile
perjuries than with these fanatic spirits.[8]

James appointed a group of bishops to have overall superintendence of the Scottish church and to sit in Parliament. By this means he asserted royal authority of a church which remained, in all other respects, Presbyterian.

The Hampton Court Conference

The English Puritan leaders who hastened to meet with the king doubtless considered it a smart move to strike while the iron was hot – to show their loyalty and present their case before James's mind could be poisoned by episcopal prejudice. Most of them were moderate men who were not tarred with the Presbyterian brush and did not seek a politico-religious settlement that would weaken the position of the Crown, but their enthusiastic initiative or James's inability to distinguish between them and the "Melvillites" meant that the two parties got off on the wrong foot.

The king welcomed the Millenary Petition. He was flattered to be invited to sort out the religious differences within his new kingdom. He would, he decided, begin his reign with a gracious irenical initiative to bring peace and unity to his subjects. He pondered the petition during his leisurely southward progress during the summer and it was while he was staying with the earl of Pembroke in his Wiltshire home, Wilton House, on 29–30 August 1603 that he gave orders for a meeting, "for the hearing, and for the determining, things pretended to be amiss in the church".

Those agitating for a review of the state of the English church would have done well to heed the word "pretended". It suggested at the very least that the new king was not prepared to take their complaints at face value. However, the optimism of the Puritans was unbounded. Throughout the autumn their network buzzed with excited anticipation. At last, the malcontents believed they were to be provided with a forum to air their grievances about the Prayer Book, Anglican vestments, and a raft of "popish" rituals and customs to which they objected. They were in for a rude shock.

James celebrated Christmas with considerable festivity at Hampton Court and convened his ecclesiastical conference there on 14 January. The invitation list must have made his intentions clear to those who were hoping that the gathering would be a major step forward along the path of church reform. The septuagenarian Archbishop Whitgift led the delegation but he was now infirm (he died in March) and the de facto episcopal spokesman was the archbishop-in-waiting, Richard Bancroft, bishop of London. His hostility towards the Puritans was well known. As early as 1588 he had denounced them as people "by whom her majesty is depraved, her authority is impugned... civil government is called in question".[9] During the conference even the king felt the need to rebuke Bancroft for his intemperate language. Seven other bishops (those of Durham, Winchester, Worcester, Chichester, Carlisle, Peterborough, and St David's) made up the episcopal team and, in addition, there were five cathedral deans (including Lancelot Andrewes of Westminster). Members of the privy council were eligible to attend as observers. These were all establishment Anglicans and, for the most part, men noted for their scholarship and diligence in the performance of their duties.

Four Puritan spokesmen were brought in to face this formidable array of power and talent. John Reynolds (or Rainolds), president of Corpus Christi College, Oxford, a scholar of distinction and a minister, was recognized as their "foreman". Laurence Chaderton, Master of Emmanuel College, Cambridge, was a noted expert in Hebrew and Greek and one of the most famous preachers of his day. "Once when he held forth for two hours and then proposed to trespass no longer on his hearers' patience the [congregation] cried out 'For God's sake, Sir, go on, go on!' "[10] John Knewstub, rector of Cockfield, Suffolk, and fellow of St John's College, Cambridge, was a noted controversialist who wrote against Anabaptists and other heretics on the radical fringe as well as Catholics and

Anglican ceremonialists. The fourth member of the Puritan team, Thomas Sparke, was a minister in Lincolnshire. Though "in great esteem for his learning", he made no impact whatsoever on the conference. According to a contemporary chronicler, Sparke "spoke not one word" and was so overawed by the king that he did a doctrinal U-turn and "did… yield himself in his practice to universal conformity".[11] The quartet chosen by James to put forward the argument for continued reformation were by no means the most outspoken critics of the Anglican settlement. They were either moderates or controversialists not noted for their debating skills. The king had deliberately staged a confrontation between the league champions and a second division team.

Before we can consider the progress of the Hampton Court Conference it is necessary to offer a word of caution. For our knowledge of this gathering we are almost entirely dependent on the official report of it. The work of drawing this up was entrusted to William Barlow, then dean of Chester. If there had ever been any intention of producing an impartial account of proceedings, Barlow would certainly not have been the man to be chosen for the job. He was partisan and a time-server (see pp. 95–96). The Puritans complained afterwards not only that he had misrepresented them, but that he had given the impression that they and the king were at odds. His narrative certainly made James appear erudite, witty, and perhaps more anti-Puritan than he actually was. It was Barlow, for example, who credited the king with warning Reynolds and Co. that, if they did not behave themselves, he would "harry them out of the land or do worse".

That said, the conference was always going to be an unequal contest and the junior position of the Puritans was underlined on the first day when they were left to their own devices in an anteroom while James opened proceedings and went on to discuss certain doctrinal issues with his bishops. Reynolds and his friends might have been glad to be out of earshot for James's inaugural speech:

> *Blessed be God's gracious goodness, who hath brought me*
> *into the promised Land, where religion is purely professed,*

> *where I sit amongst grave, learned and reverend men, not*
> *as before, elsewhere, a king without state, without honour,*
> *without order, where beardless boys would brave us to the*
> *face... Our purpose therefore is, like a good physician, to*
> *examine and try the complaints, and fully to remove the*
> *occasions thereof, if scandalous; cure them, if dangerous;*
> *and take knowledge of them, if frivolous, thereby to cast a*
> *sop into Cerberus's mouth, that he bark no more.*[12]

It was by no means flattering for critics of the *status quo* to be compared to the three-headed dog who guarded the gates of hell.

When the Puritans were admitted to the privy chamber on the second day they found James accompanied by nine-year-old Prince Henry (doubtless included to witness the humiliation of the presumptuous dissidents) and flanked by his bishops. The king, ably seconded by Bancroft, enjoyed demolishing the arguments of the Puritans. Every issue they brought up he flatly rejected. Reynolds and his companions became the unwilling victims of the king's revenge for all the indignities he had suffered at the hands of Scottish Presbyterians. James enjoyed himself hugely. In a later letter he exulted, "They fled me from argument to argument."

However, on one issue the king did agree with Reynolds. The minister asked, "May your Majesty be pleased to direct that the Bible be new translated, such versions as are extant not answering to the original."[13] It was a strange initiative to come from the Puritan party. The Geneva Bible, with its strongly Calvinist glosses, was still the most popular version in current use. To see it superseded by a royally approved translation which would certainly be devoid of doctrinal notes looked like a tactical blunder on the part of the Puritan delegates. This may have come home to them pointedly when James eagerly responded. "I could never yet see a Bible well-translated in English," he said,

> *but I think that of all, that of Geneva is the worst.*
> *I wish some special pains were taken for an uniform*
> *translation; which should be done by the best learned in*

both universities, then reviewed by the bishops, presented
to the privy council, lastly ratified by royal authority, to be
read in the whole church, and no other.[14]

Bancroft, who had hitherto scorned the suggestion of yet another English Bible, now suddenly decided that it was a splendid idea. So everyone was agreed.

How are we to read between the lines of this exchange? I suspect that Reynolds knew of James's antipathy to the Geneva Bible. The king's Presbyterian mentors had been adept at quoting chapter and verse to demonstrate the limited power of earthly rulers and the duty of subjects to reject them if their conscience so dictated. This was one of the thorny moral and political issues of the time. Calvin had urged unconditional obedience to the civil magistrate as God's representative. In this he was followed by James I. But in the wake of the St Bartholomew's Day Massacre (1572) when thousands of French Protestants were put to the sword by royal order, Calvin's successor at Geneva, Theodore Beza, had modified the official Calvinist line. It was this revisionist thinking which influenced the later editions of the Geneva Bible and, during the turbulent religious wars which marked the late sixteenth century, most Protestants had moved to a position which sanctioned resistance on grounds of conscience.

James had made no secret of his dissatisfaction with the glosses of the Geneva Bible which ran contrary to his concept of absolute monarchy. Reynolds must have known, or at least guessed, that the king was bent on getting rid of the Geneva Bible. The Bishops' Bible had failed to provide an attractive substitute. The logical corollary was to set forth a new translation. By actually putting forth the suggestion himself Reynolds staked a claim for Puritan scholars to be involved in the project.

But we may be wrong in detecting such a subtle plan. Reynolds was also a theologian and, as such, he was aware of the shortcomings of the Geneva Bible. It was over forty years since the book had first made its appearance and, in that time, major changes had occurred in the world of biblical scholarship. In particular, Catholic and

Protestant linguists had extended their understanding of the Bible's original languages. One monumental result was the *Royal Antwerp Polyglot*, an eight-volume work completed in 1572 which printed the text in parallel columns of Hebrew, Chaldaic, Greek, and Latin. Philip II of Spain had brought together the finest Catholic scholars to work on the project. In addition to the texts, readers were offered Hebrew, Aramaic, Syriac, and Greek grammars and lexicons. In 1580 Immanuel Tremellius published the last volume of a Latin translation from Hebrew and Syriac texts. Tremellius was an Italian Jew who had converted first to Catholicism and subsequently to Calvinism. His colourful career had involved spells as Regius Professor of Hebrew at Cambridge and professor of Old Testament Studies at Heidelberg. Theodore Beza also produced a Latin New Testament based on his own reading of ancient texts. The labours of these masters inspired a whole generation of biblical scholars and Reynolds was, in all probability, among those who, party issues aside, wanted to see an English Bible which was as accurate as it could possibly be. The existing situation was unsatisfactory to many. People had a choice between the Bishops' Bible, which was neutral, dull, and not free from error, and the more accurate but partisan Geneva Bible. Even fair-minded Puritans could see the desirability of a "tidying-up" policy.

Planning the New Translation

Thus was set in hand the first English Bible whose production was, theoretically at least, overseen by the head of state. Since the sovereign was concerned, the book had to be good. There must be no risk of a second Bishops' Bible. All the best available brains must be pressed into service on the project. In a letter to Bancroft, who, despite his original hesitation about the scheme, now became its coordinator, James wrote:

> ... *we require you to move all our bishops to inform themselves of all such learned men within their several*

dioceses, as have special skill in the Hebrew and Greek tongues, have taken pains, in their private study of the Scriptures, for the clearing of any obscurities either in the Hebrew or in the Greek, or touching any difficulties or mistakings in the former English translation, which we have now commanded to be thoroughly viewed and amended, and thereupon to write unto them, earnestly charging them, and signifying our pleasure therein, that they send such their observations either to Mr. Lively, our Hebrew reader in Cambridge, or to Dr. Harding, our Hebrew reader in Oxford, or to Dr. Andrews, dean of Westminster, to be imparted to the rest of their several companies; so that our said intended translation may have the help and furtherance of all our principal learned men within this our kingdom.[15]

The king did not, in fact, wait for his new archbishop to assemble a team of translators. By the summer of 1604 he had personally designated fifty-four scholars to be involved (by the time work commenced the actual number employed appears to have fallen to forty-seven for reasons unknown). It might be thought that to involve "all our principal learned men" was a certain way of ensuring that the project lost itself for all time in the impenetrable jungle of academic debate. James was alive to this danger; he had already informed Bancroft that "so religious a work should admit of no delay" and that the chief translators "should with all possible speed meet together". He demanded frequent progress reports from Bancroft, who in turn chivvied the scholars. The work was divided among six teams, each of between seven and ten men. The teams were gathered together at Cambridge, Oxford, and Westminster, and there they remained until their task was accomplished. They received no payment for their labours but, to prevent any of his scholars falling into penury over "so religious a work", the king provided rich livings for those not already beneficed.

The king left absolutely nothing to chance. He supervised the drawing up of a list of very precise guidelines:

1. *The ordinary Bible read in the church, commonly called the* Bishops' Bible, *to be followed, and as little altered as the truth of the original will permit.*

2. *The names of the prophets, and the holy writers, with the other names of the text, to be retained, as nigh as may be, accordingly as they were vulgarly used.*

3. *The old ecclesiastical words to be kept, viz. the word* church *not to be translated* congregation, *etc.*

4. *When a word hath divers significations, that to be kept which hath been most commonly used by the most of the ancient fathers, being agreeable to the propriety of the place and the analogy of the faith.*

5. *The division of the chapters to be altered, either not at all, or as little as may be, if necessity so require.*

6. *No marginal notes at all to be affixed, but only for the explanation of the Hebrew or Greek words, which cannot without some circumlocution, so briefly and fitly be expressed in the text.*

7. *Such quotations of places to be marginally set down as shall serve for the fit reference of one scripture to another.*

8. *Every particular man of each company, to take the same chapter, or chapters, and having translated or amended them severally by himself, where he thinketh good, all to meet together, confer what they have done, and agree for their parts what shall stand.*

9. *As any one company hath dispatched any one book in this manner they shall send it to the rest, to be considered of seriously and judiciously for his majesty is very careful in this point.*

10. *If any company, upon the review of the book so sent, doubt or*

differ upon any place, to send them word thereof; note the place, and withal send the reasons to which if they consent not the difference to be compounded at the general meeting, which is to be of the chief persons of each company, at the end of the work.

11. *When any place of special obscurity is doubted of letters to be directed, by authority, to send to any learned man in the land, for his judgment of such a place.*

12. *Letters to be sent from every bishop to the rest of his clergy, admonishing them of this translation in hand; and to move and charge as many as being skilful in the tongues; and having taken pains in that kind, to send his particular observations to the company, either at Westminster, Cambridge or Oxford.*

13. *The directors in each company, to be the deans of Westminster and Chester for that place; and the king's professors in the Hebrew or Greek in either university.*

14. *These translations to be used when they agree better with the text than the Bishops' Bible: Tyndale's, Matthew's, Coverdale's, Whitchurch's [The Great Bible], Geneva.*

15. *Besides the said directors before mentioned, three or four of the most ancient and grave divines, in either of the universities, not employed in translating, to be assigned by the vice-chancellor, upon conference with the rest of the heads, to be overseers of the translations as well Hebrew as Greek, for the better observation of the fourth rule above specified.*[16]

CHAPTER 5

THE GOOD HAND OF
THE LORD UPON US

When, in 1937, the Revised Standard Version of the Bible was set in hand, its projectors aimed to provide a translation which would "embody the best results of modern scholarship as to the meaning of the Scriptures, and express this meaning in English diction which is designed for use in private and public worship".[1] The objectives of the twentieth-century translators were the same as those of their seventeenth-century predecessors – and, indeed, of most scholars who have ever set in hand a major revision of the English Bible. The objective is easy to state; its achievement is less so.

Any translation of ancient texts has to be anchored in both the past and the present: in the past because it has a duty to represent as accurately as possible the message of the original authors; in the present because it must be intelligible to contemporaries. This is by no means straightforward and becomes more difficult when the "text" in question is the library of ancient poetry, chronicles, law, philosophy, biography, letters, and prophecy which makes up the Holy Bible. All of those involved in creating the new version believed that Scripture was God-breathed and undertook their task with the appropriate seriousness and diligence. The rigid procedure of checking and double-checking imposed by the king was designed to reduce human error to a minimum. But the translators were only men and inevitably they brought to the work the baggage of their own opinions, prejudices, and intellectual limitations. The only real qualification for inclusion in the team was theological and linguistic expertise. England could not boast a large number of scholars with the necessary knowledge so it was inevitable that the group would include men of wide-ranging abilities and opinions. Academics and particularly academic theologians are not noted for frictionless concord and it is not remotely likely that the makers of the King James Version achieved their task without argument. Sadly we have no accounts of any of the hundreds of meetings held between 1604 and 1611. All we can do is identify some of the participants and use our imaginations to consider how they might have got on together.

The Translation Committees

Six teams were set up, two each at Westminster, Oxford and Cambridge. The text was apportioned to them as follows:

WESTMINSTER I: GENESIS – II KINGS

WESTMINSTER II: NEW TESTAMENT EPISTLES

OXFORD I: ISAIAH – MALACHI

OXFORD II: THE GOSPELS, ACTS, AND REVELATION

CAMBRIDGE I: I CHRONICLES – SONG OF SOLOMON

CAMBRIDGE II: APOCRYPHA

The leader of Westminster I, and undoubtedly the doyen of all the translators, was Lancelot Andrewes. Andrewes was a complex character, made up of almost contradictory dispositions. He was a stern ascetic who rose early and devoted six hours every morning to prayer and study. Many of his prayers were published posthumously and have enriched public and private Anglican devotion over the years. At the same time he was a skilled administrator who attended assiduously to business in all the successive offices he held. He was indifferent to personal advancement while, at the same time, an eager frequenter of the royal court and seeker of patronage. As a result of his popularity with Elizabeth I and James I, Andrewes became dean of Westminster (1601), bishop of Chichester (1605), bishop of Ely (1609), and bishop of Winchester (1619). In his personal relationships with men of all parties he was tolerant and generous. Yet he was, in his time, the great Anglican controversialist who set his face against Catholics and Puritans and was a member of the tribunal which, in 1611, condemned the last radical heretic to be burned at Smithfield. Andrewes was a prodigious scholar. He was said to have mastered at least fifteen languages. One contemporary quipped that, had Andrewes been around at the time of the building of the Tower of Babel where God bestowed different languages on humankind, Andrewes would have earned a fortune as an interpreter. He thought deeply about many contemporary issues facing the Church and pronounced on them in books and sermons. Yet the greater part of his literary output was not published until after his death.

A member of his team whom Andrewes may have found difficult to handle was Dr John Overall. Overall was the Regius Professor of Divinity at Cambridge and a prickly customer who enjoyed a scrap. In 1597 he had been appointed Master of St Catherine's College but only after a bitterly fought election and – in the opinion of some – the securing of influence at court. Two years later Overall was in trouble again, this time on the more serious matter of promoting heresy in his lectures. The more pronounced Calvinists among his colleagues (including Laurence Chaderton of Emmanuel) objected to Overall's teaching on repentance, grace, and private confession.

When called to account by the vice chancellor, he repeatedly put off confronting his accusers and, when he, at last did so, gave way to a display of shouting and personal abuse. The bad-tempered dispute rumbled on for months.

Its central issue was not confined to Cambridge. Indeed, what divided men like Overall and Chaderton was dividing the whole Protestant world. It was the quarrel over Arminianism and it was not a new theological problem. Scholars had for centuries applied themselves to what was a central paradox of the faith: how can God be all-powerful and all-loving? If he desires all men to be saved why does he not arrange it so that they are? If some of his creatures resist his grace, then his power must be limited. Calvin had taken the sovereignty of God as his starting point. The divine will cannot be thwarted. Therefore, the distinction between the saved and the damned can only be explained by *election* – God preordains those who are destined for heaven and hell.

Jacob Arminius of Leiden challenged this conventional Calvinist position. Individual salvation, he asserted, was dependent, not on election by a sovereign God whose eternal purposes were as inscrutable as they were inescapable, but on willing response to a loving God who desired all men to be saved. Arminius's teaching was attractive to the authorities. The practical problem created by strict Calvinism was that it encouraged the existence of rival leadership within the church. The "elect" constituted themselves a spiritual elite, the chosen of the Lord. It followed, in their thinking, that those who opposed them – whether bishops, archbishops, or king – must belong to the synagogues of Satan. Such an attitude was as hubristic as it was disruptive and could not be tolerated.

Richard Thomson, another member of the Westminster I team, was a convinced Arminian but that was not the only thing that other clerics had against him. He was a fellow of Clare College, Cambridge, and a brilliant linguist. He had been born in Holland, travelled widely on the continent, and mastered several modern as well as ancient languages. When in England he seems to have preferred the London social scene where Shakespeare, Ben Jonson, and Thomas Dekker drew large audiences to the playhouses and the young bucks of the Jacobean court set the tone of conspicuous consumption and display. William Prynne (1600–69) later described Thomson as a "debauched, drunken English Dutchman who seldom went one night to bed sober".[2] But Prynne was a fierce critic of the Stuart court and its personnel and he was only thirteen when Thomson died. However, it must be significant that one of Thomson's classical heroes, whose works he edited, was the Epicurean poet Martial, who, in his day, had a reputation for sycophancy and obscenity. Thomson was probably the youngest of the translators, being in his mid-thirties at the time of the Hampton Court Conference. Another somewhat exotic character on Andrewes's team was Hadrian Saravia. He was of mixed Spanish and Flemish parentage and had ended up in England as a result of religious persecution in the Low Countries. Lancelot Andrewes took the refugee under his wing and encouraged him to engage in written controversy with Beza. It is scarcely surprising to discover that his principal work was a defence of episcopacy. However, Saravia was no contentious academic. According to one contemporary, he was "most anxious and earnest in seeking for general peace and concord in the church of God".[3]

The most original genius attracted to the Westminster I team was William Bedwell. He was a Cambridge graduate but did not follow an academic career and may have come to the attention of the establishment because of his uncle, who was master of the ordnance in the Tower of London. Bedwell was one of the marvels of the age. He excelled as both a mathematician and a linguist. He was master of the original Bible languages but it was as the leading exponent of Arabic culture and literature that he was most famous. At a time when most Christians were content to consign to the devil all the people of the Islamic world, Bedwell was fascinated by the scholarship of the great medieval Arab doctors, mathematicians, and philosophers. He brought to the study of the Old Testament texts a fresh understanding of the cultural life of the Holy Land.

Westminster II was led by William Barlow, whom we have already briefly encountered. He was an establishment man through and through and one of the most hated churchmen of his day.

By 1604 his career was in full flood. He had commended himself to Archbishop Whitgift, whose chaplain he became in 1597, and through him won the favour of Queen Elizabeth. He knew how to preach pleasing sermons and his smarmy manner won him preferment. There seems no doubt that in his report on the Hampton Court Conference Barlow deliberately flattered the king and that he exaggerated James's support for the episcopal party and his hostility towards the Puritans. His preface to the report was a particularly obnoxious piece of sycophancy. If the ambitious dean of Chester regarded *The Summe and Substance of the Conference at Hampton Court* as a golden opportunity to court royal favour, he did not miscalculate. He was appointed to fill the next vacancy on the episcopal bench and became bishop of Rochester in May 1606. Two years later he was elevated to the more prestigious diocese of Lincoln. In the politico-religious conflicts of the next few years Barlow was often wheeled out as a leading government propagandist. From the pulpit, in the House of Lords, and in pamphlets he staunchly defended the establishment. He was not reputed a great scholar but made a reasonable fist of translating Romans and Jude.

Barlow was seconded on Westminster II by John Spenser, sometime reader in Greek at Corpus Christi College, Oxford. In 1607 he succeeded Reynolds as President of the college but theologically he was a horse of a very different colour. His close friendship with Richard Hooker and his important work as editor of Hooker's *Laws of Ecclesiastical Polity* mark him out as very much an establishment man. In 1604 he held the rich living of St Sepulchre's, Newgate. This made it easy for him to attend committee meetings.

If the Westminster teams had a strongly establishment flavour the same could not be said of their counterparts in the university cities. Edward Lively, Regius Professor of Hebrew at Cambridge, was appointed leader of Cambridge I but after his death within months of taking up the position, Laurence Chaderton became its leading light. Master of the recently-founded Puritan college of Emmanuel, he was a much-loved scholar, so modest that his arm had to be twisted to persuade him to take up the Mastership. The corpulent John Richardson was a colleague of Chaderton's at Emmanuel but his theological position shifted when he became Regius Professor of Divinity (1607) and, successively, Master of Peterhouse (1608) and master of Trinity (1615). His students referred to him scornfully as "a fat-bellied Arminian". No such backsliders were Andrew Byng, Regius Professor of Hebrew from 1608, Thomas Harrison, and Francis Dillingham. They were Puritans and outstanding Hebraists. Their knowledge of Old Testament language and literature was invaluable to a team called upon to render into English some of the Bible's finest poetry – Job, the Song of Solomon, and, above all, the Psalms. It was a daunting task to reinvent these Old Testament hymns. Coverdale's English psalter was already well known and loved by three generations of worshippers. But few would disagree that the new rendering often achieved an immediacy and fluency lacking in Coverdale's translation. The older version in the Great Bible and the Book of Common Prayer opened Psalm 23 with,

> *The Lord is my shepherd: therefore can I lack nothing.*
> *He shall feed me in a green pasture: and lead me*
> *forth beside the waters of comfort.*
> *He shall convert my soul: and bring me forth*
> *in the paths of righteousness, for his Name's sake.*

Chaderton's team gave us the words which have entered the very soul of English Christianity,

> *The Lord is my shepherd; I shall not want.*
> *He maketh me to lie down in green pastures: he leadeth*
> *me beside the still waters.*
> *He restoreth my soul: he leadeth me in the paths*
> *of righteousness for his name's sake.*

The scholar in charge of Cambridge II was Dr John Duport, Master of Jesus College and one of the most respected seniors of the university. He was also an outspoken champion of mainline Calvinism. In 1595 he had joined with Chaderton and six other heads of colleges to send a letter of protest to the archbishop about the infiltration of those doctrines which would soon be labelled as "Arminian". They intended, as they said, "to testify our own opinions for the defence and preservation of that truth of doctrine in some substantial points which hath been always in our memories both here and elsewhere, taught, professed and continued, and never openly impugned amongst us but by some persons of late".[4] The central point of controversy was the old one of election. Could any Christian feel *totally* confident of his salvation, despite his own frequent lapses into sin? A substantial body of senior academics at Cambridge had no doubt on the matter.

Not all Puritans possessed the serene self-assurance of a Chaderton or a Duport. Sidney Sussex College, Cambridge, preserves a diary of Samuel Ward, who was Master of the college from 1610 to 1643. In 1604 he became one of the younger members of the Cambridge II team (he had received his MA in 1596). His diary covers the years 1595–99, when he was a fellow of Emmanuel. It is an introspective document concerned largely with the writer's devotional life and is revealing about the religious atmosphere in the university. Ward found the spiritual pace set by Chaderton exhausting. He was less than captivated by the Master's sermons and even fell asleep during one of them (a useful counterbalance to the story of that other occasion when Chaderton's hearers begged him, "In God's name, Sir, go on."). Ward struggled with the sins of gluttony and sloth – or, at least, his possibly oversensitive conscience accused him of those failings. His guilt at the "overmuch delight" in the "transitory pleasures of this world" was a cross he carried daily. One can only assume that it found positive outlet in energetic application to the translation of the Apocrypha when he was a few years older. Ward went on to enjoy a distinguished career as Lady Margaret's Professor of Divinity and a prolific author. At the end of his days, despite his religious leanings, he was unable to side against King Charles I in the Civil War and spent some months in prison.

We are given only partial glimpses of the daily life of those engaged in making the King James Version. The chief exception is another member of Cambridge II, Dr John Bois (or Boys). He made notes of the routine meetings of the committee and we can amplify these by referring to a brief manuscript biography written by a close friend, Anthony Walker. All this is doubly fortuitous because Bois was not one of the leading academics or upwardly mobile senior clergy of the day and we might otherwise know nothing about him. He had been a fellow of St John's College but resigned on his marriage in 1596. Thereafter, he lived most of his life as the struggling incumbent of a country parish (Boxworth). Bois was an introverted and hypochondriac soul. He abandoned his early resolve to become a physician because his reading of medical books convinced him that he had most of the ailments described. He was one of those dedicated clergy so committed to his work that he neglected his own well-being. He was a conscientious preacher and a selfless pastor. He and his wife had to take in lodgers to make ends meet. Quite how or why, as a non-university resident, he was selected for the translation team is not clear but it gave him respite from his parochial duties.

Every Monday he would ride the five miles to Cambridge. There he applied himself diligently to his task. Through the daylight hours he wrestled with the Hebrew text and compared the various translations available in English and Latin as well as some of the continental versions. Six days of the week were spent in reading, writing, and laying the groundwork for his translation. Only on Saturday evening was he allowed to ride back to Boxford to discharge his sabbath duties to his parishioners. Bois was so hard-working that he was the first to finish his allotted task. He even assisted one of his more laggard brethren who was falling behind. After two years of private study Bois settled to the actual writing of the new text in close collaboration with his colleagues. The team members met frequently to compare notes. Each would read out the section he had just completed to his colleagues, who would follow the recitation carefully, referring all the time to other translations and stopping the reader when they had comments or suggestions to make. It was, doubtless, Bois's industry and dedication that recommended him as one of the six translators to go to London in 1610 for the final revision stage. It would be pleasant to be able to record that Bois's dedication won him recognition and reward, but unlike several of his co-workers, he was no ambitious, self-promoting ecclesiastic and the highest point he reached on the ladder of preferment was a prebendary of Ely.

The leader of Oxford I, John Reynolds, we have already met. He was the man who had set the whole translation project in motion. He was one of the most prodigious scholars of his day. It was said of him, "He alone was a well-furnished library, full of all faculties, of all studies, of all learning; the memory, the reading of that man were near to a miracle."[5] He was also a sick man. Tuberculosis was reducing him to little more than a skeleton before his colleagues' eyes. But he did not plead infirmity to have his share of the burden reduced. On the contrary, he may be said to have become a martyr to the King James Version. He beavered away at his own portions of the Prophets and, once a week, received his co-workers in his rooms at Corpus Christi College to compare notes and arrive at agreed readings. He died on 21 May 1607 at the age of fifty-seven. In his will he had little to leave in the way of worldly goods except his books, which were distributed among his university friends. In his work on the Bible, Reynolds was ably supported by Thomas Holland, the Regius Professor of Divinity (described by one contemporary as "mighty in the Scriptures") and by the firm Protestants Richard Kilbye and Richard Brett, both of Lincoln College.

The atmosphere of Oxford II was markedly different. It was dominated by two singularly unattractive men. "By the help of Jesus, I will not leave one preacher in my diocese who doth not subscribe and conform." So vowed Thomas Ravis on his appointment as bishop of London in 1607. He had already established his anti-Puritan credentials in his earlier roles as dean of Christ Church College (1596–1605) and bishop of Gloucester (1605–7). He was balanced on the committee by the equally unyielding Puritan divine, George Abbot, Master of University College. He was as formidable in preaching and teaching (he once delivered a course of 260 sermons on the book of Jonah) as he was in seeking out any vestige of "popery". He caused a bonfire to be made of "idolatrous" pictures and mercilessly attacked personally any who betrayed leanings towards Arminianism. Strangely, King James liked him and in 1611 Abbot was appointed archbishop of Canterbury.

After all these clerical wranglings and rivalries, it is pleasing to be able to conclude this introduction to some of the more interesting translators with a brief account of the only layman among them. If any man deserved the description of scholar and educator, that man was Sir Henry Savile. On leaving Oxford, where he had achieved a glowing reputation, he travelled widely before returning to take up the posts of Warden of Merton College and Latin secretary to Queen Elizabeth. But his heart was in education and he campaigned to be appointed Provost of Eton College. There he dedicated himself to teaching and to preparing an edition of the works of St Chrysostom, an ambitious enterprise. His knowledge of the classical languages was prodigious and he was widely acknowledged as the most learned student of profane literature the age produced.

These, then, were the leading lights of that diverse body of learned men who were brought together to produce a new English translation of the Holy Bible. Although they spent long hours cloistered together in stuffy college rooms or musty libraries they did not do their work in a vacuum. During the years that they were employed on their exacting task, the world moved on and they could not be immune to change.

Church and State under James I

James I had "ascended the English throne a cautious man, merely thanking God that he could now let himself go in the matter of expenditure".[6] The king from across the border believed that his new realm was richer than it was. Expenditure on the royal household doubled as soon as James ascended the throne. He was extravagant both in indulging his own passions and in offering bountiful rewards to his favourites. The court in London was filled with James's Scottish cronies – a state of affairs that did not go down well with the leaders of England's ancient aristocratic families. All this might have been tolerable had the new court set a serious and dignified tone. It actually did just the opposite. Celebrity-watchers had a vision of things to come in 1606 when James's brother-in-law, Christian IV of Denmark, paid a state visit to London. According to the ne'er-do-well gossip and scribbler Sir John Harington, court entertainments descended into drunken orgies which left the royal apartments strewn with the debris of extravagant feasting and vomit. The man who presided over this chaos was the king whom sycophantic bishops eulogized as a paragon of Christian virtue. From quite early in the reign statesmen and churchmen who shook their heads in despair at such distasteful goings-on consoled themselves with the prospect of better things to come. The teenage Prince Henry was a young man of strong character and impeccable Protestant beliefs. By the time the new Bible saw the light of day, he had established a rival court which attracted men of a serious disposition. Sadly, hope for the future was dashed the following year (1612), when the prince died suddenly of typhoid.

Maintaining the elaborate Stuart court cost money and for that the king had to approach Parliament. Thus began that long conflict between Crown and Commons which would end in civil war. In 1614 James told the Spanish ambassador,

> *The House of Commons is a body without a head.*
> *The members give their opinions in a disorderly manner.*
> *At their meetings nothing is heard but cries, shouts and*
> *confusion. I am surprised that my ancestors should ever*
> *have permitted such an institution to come into existence.*
> *But I am a stranger, and found it here when I arrived, so*
> *that I am obliged to put up with what I cannot get rid of.*[7]

Frustration was felt just as keenly by many parliamentarians. Several constitutional and political issues which had arisen in the previous reign remained unresolved – religion, foreign affairs, money. The Commons wanted the laws against Catholics rigidly enforced, especially after the Gunpowder Plot of November 1605. James wavered, sometimes exhibiting firmness, sometimes leniency. He was in a difficult position because his own wife was a Catholic. One of the king's first acts was to end the long, debilitating war with Spain. This was widely welcomed but when he began negotiations for a marriage alliance with the leading Catholic power, many thought he was going too far. Yet it was always money which was the focus of mistrust between the sovereign and the legislature. James's first parliament lasted until 1610 but when it failed to grant him sufficient taxation he dissolved it and tried to survive on prerogative income (i.e. revenue from sources such as excise duties which did not require parliamentary sanction). This proved inadequate and the king summoned his second assembly in 1614. Such were the disagreements between Crown and Commons that it lasted less than two months and was dubbed the "Addled Parliament". At about this time someone circulated an anonymous pamphlet which proposed the calling of annual parliaments as a constant check on the powers of the sovereign.

In the religious life of the country the dominant strain was anti-Catholicism. The bulk of James's subjects were suspicious of the covert Catholics in their midst and the influence of Rome and Madrid. The bitter fifteen-year war with Spain had come to an end but a state of cold war still existed. Spain was widely regarded as *the* enemy. James, ever determined to play the role of peacemaker, married his daughter Elizabeth to the Calvinist Frederick V of the Palatinate while seeking a union for his heir with a Spanish princess. This was his way of striking an admirable balance in international affairs. That was not how his Protestant subjects saw things. They mistrusted any move towards reconciliation with the Catholic powers. Such policy initiatives were linked in their minds with the introduction of ecclesiastical vestments, excessive ritual, and ornate church decoration – all were signs of a Romeward drift. Unfortunately for them, they could not present a united front. English Protestantism was increasingly divided. Anglicans and

Puritans were at odds. Calvinists and Arminians were in conflict. There was a growing tendency for Arminianism and "high church" Anglicanism to cohere. Later in the century Charles I was asked what the Arminians held. He replied, "The best bishoprics and deaneries in England." That trend had already begun by 1611. The momentum of the Reformation was weakening. The ecclesiastical establishment was striving to contain it. Bancroft, Andrewes, and their colleagues no longer regarded Anglican doctrine as resting on Luther's twin pillars of *sola fidei* and *sola scriptura*.[8] This was the background against which the King James Version came into being and, inevitably, it bore the marks of contemporary conflicts and compromises.

The Publication of the King James Version

The translators' brief had been to revise the Bishops' Bible by reference to the best Greek and Hebrew texts. In fact, they went far beyond their brief, referring to every available version in their search for the best variant readings. One might have supposed that the large number of "cooks" involved would have spoiled the broth; that there could not possibly have emerged any unity of language or style from the labours of such a heterogeneous band of scholars. This problem had, however, been foreseen. When, after four painstaking years, the basic revision work was over, all the scripts were subjected to a final editorial process. Early in 1610 two members of each team assembled in Stationers' Hall, London, to review the entire revision. This final checking stage took nine months more out of the scholars' lives but it is gratifying to learn that they were now more adequately recompensed. Each of them received thirty shillings per week from the Stationers' Company in order to defray his expenses in the capital. It was only in the autumn of that year that the finally approved manuscript went to the printer.

The work was provided with a sickeningly sycophantic dedicatory epistle which began,

Great and manifold were the blessings, dread sovereign,
which Almighty God, the Father of all mercies, bestowed
upon us, the people of England, when first he sent Your
Majesty's Royal Person to rule and reign over us...

The encouragement of true religion, the writer assured the king,

hath so bound and firmly knit the hearts of all Your
Majesty's loyal and religious people unto You that Your
very name is precious among Them ... and they bless
You in their hearts as that sanctified Person who, under
God is the immediate Author of their true Happiness.

Above all, the writer declared, James was to be applauded for commissioning the new translation and maintaining a close interest in its progress. "Your Majesty did never desist to urge and to excite those to whom it was committed."

The anonymous writer of this dedicatory epistle has sometimes been identified as Thomas Bilson, bishop of Winchester. He was another of those career ecclesiastics with whom we have by now become familiar. During the latter years of Elizabeth's reign he had spent more time at court than in attending to his pastoral duties. He had commended himself to the queen, largely by his forceful defence of the religious establishment. He was made bishop of Worcester in 1596 while he was still in his forties. Then, within less than a year the more prestigious diocese of Winchester fell into his lap.

His haughtiness was well revealed in his reaction when he was told about the forthcoming Hampton Court Conference. He tried to dissuade the king from inviting any of the Puritan ministers, so that "bishops (being esteemed the fathers and pillars of the Church, for gravity, learning and government...) might not be so disparaged as to confer with men of so mean place and quality".[9] Bilson played no part in the work of translation but he was a member of the final revision team. It is difficult to imagine him as being greatly concerned with the quality of the translation. Just as he had no great reputation as a scholar, so he took no clear side in any of the theological disputes of the day. He seems to have been too busy winning himself a position on the privy council and accumulating those perks and sinecures that enabled him to die a very wealthy man.

The new Bible was also provided with another introductory essay altogether more worthy of our attention. Miles Smith, who wrote a preface entitled *The Translators to the Reader*, could scarcely have been more different from Bilson. He had earned his place on the Oxford I team because of his expertise in oriental languages. It was said of him that "Chaldaic, Syriac and Arabic were as familiar to him almost as his own native tongue".[10] Smith was one of the final revisers and, presumably, a member of the delegation that proffered a presentation copy to James. Smith's preface explained the brief he and his colleagues had been given. He reassured readers that the intention had not been to produce a new translation but to review the existing versions and "out of many good ones [to make] one principal good one". Any eulogizing in his essay Smith kept for the sacred text itself. It is, he suggested,

> *a whole armoury of weapons, both offensive, and defensive, whereby we may save our selves and put the enemy to flight. It is not an herb, but a tree, or rather a whole paradise of trees of life, which bring forth fruit every month, and the fruit thereof is for meat, and the leaves for medicine. It is not a pot of Manna, or a cruse of oil, which were for memory only, or for a meal's meat or two, but as it were a shower of heavenly bread sufficient for a whole host, be it never so great; and as it were a whole cellar full of oil vessels; whereby all our necessities may be provided for, and our debts discharged. In a word, it is... a fountain of most pure water springing up unto everlasting life.*

Smith's subsequent career reveals him as a man of principle who was not afraid to stand up to royal authority. He was appointed bishop of Gloucester in 1612. However, having reached this pinnacle, Smith did not consider himself a royal mouthpiece. Rather he gave full rein to his Puritan convictions. He resisted the increased Anglican ceremonial the archbishop of Canterbury was trying to impose throughout the country. When the bishop's regime resulted in his cathedral falling into a sad state, James installed his own agent as dean with the task of beautifying the building and banning Puritan innovations such as the placing of the communion table lengthwise in the choir. The stand-off went on for several months and bitterly divided the city but the bishop's eventual defeat was inevitable.

Was the assertion in the dedicatory epistle that King James maintained a close interest in the translation work true, or just a piece of grovelling flimflam? Any attempt to establish the extent of the king's interest in the ongoing work unfortunately involves an argument from silence. There is almost no documentary evidence on the subject. Any official records that might have thrown light on it were lost in a disastrous fire which swept through Whitehall in 1698. Beyond a couple of passing references in correspondence between individual translators which allude to the king's impatience to see the work completed we have nothing on which to base a judgment except our assessment of the king's character. James was shrewd and well-informed in debate and clear-headed in reaching conclusions but, as the historian, Hugh Trevor-Roper, observed,

> *All this wisdom in the details of politics was wasted, for he never took any steps to make it practical. Instead of coping with… questions at their material roots, he studied them only in their intellectual blooms, subjecting to his judgment as an idea what might more profitably have been tackled by his statecraft as a task. As a result, the individualism in society which had begun to cause doubts at the beginning of his reign continued unchecked, except when it actually came into conflict with the prerogative of the king. Promoting each side equally, James I relied on holding the balance himself in order to*

*evade such a conflict; and then he found that he was not
permitted to do so, but remained an omniscient umpire
whom no one consulted.[11]*

James was good on theory but appalling on practice. Once the
debating was over he frequently delegated to others the implementing
of any decisions, while he moved on to think about the next problem.
This, I suspect, was what happened with the Bible project. Having
set his scholars to work, the king did not so much lose interest as
allow the project to slip down his personal agenda. This seems to be
borne out by the muddle over publication.

At long last, after an eight-year gestation, the manuscript of the
King James Version was handed over to the king's printer, Robert
Barker, towards the end of 1610. Barker must surely be considered
one of the most unfortunate characters in the long story of the
English Bible. He was the son and eventual business successor of
Christopher Barker (1529–99), who was much in favour with Queen
Elizabeth and was appointed royal printer with monopoly rights
in the publishing of statutes, royal proclamations, prayer books,
and Bibles (of all translations). Such a wide remit suggests that
the Barkers had a very profitable business but it was certainly not
without its problems. Christopher complained that Bible printing
was difficult because it was very labour intensive (and therefore
expensive) and was frequently interrupted by government work.
When a proclamation was delivered to the print works, everything
else had to be dropped and the presses turned over to the royal edict.
However, there is no doubt that Robert looked forward to getting
his hands on the manuscript being produced by the translation
team. It may well have come as a shock to learn that James I was
not prepared to pay one penny piece towards the production costs
of the great work he had set in motion. Forty years later the *Treatise
concerning the Regulating of Printing* stated,

*The sole printing of the bible and testament, with power
of restraint in others, to be of right the propriety of one
Matthew Barker… in regard that his father paid for the*

amended or corrected translation of the bible £3,500: by reason whereof the translated copy did of right belong to him and his assigns.[12]

Sadly, any such judgement came too late to save Robert Barker. He footed the bill for the new Bible and for several years had to fight against the appearance of pirate versions. Then he became involved with rival printers who contested the monopoly rights he held in certain other books. In 1635 he was committed to the King's Bench prison. He was still there when he died some nine years later.

Back in 1610 when he was dispensing large sums in wages and equipment to get the King James Version printed, Robert Barker was, understandably, in a hurry to deliver copies to the shops. This must be the reason why the book was published with undue haste. Two editions were rushed off the presses. Not only was there no uniform text; sheets from each version were bound up together. Proofreading was perfunctory. Errors and variant readings abounded. At Ruth 3:15 one version read "she [Ruth] went", while the other stated "he [Boaz] went". More alarmingly in Matthew 26:36 "Judas" was substituted for "Jesus" in one printing. Luke 23:32 recorded that Jesus was crucified along with two "other" malefactors. It would, however, be 1631 before the most notorious misprint appeared: at Exodus 20:14 the word "not" was omitted from the command "thou shalt not commit adultery". What may have upset the scholar-translators more than such typos was the dog's dinner made of the scholarly apparatus. They had spent years comparing ancient and modern texts and providing the reader with marginal notes and other devices for identifying where English words had been added to enhance the flow and where variant readings were admissible. In addition they had provided the text with chapter summaries, paragraph signs, cross references, and philological notes. When the first editions left Barker's premises, several of these aids to study were discovered to be missing or jumbled.

All in all, it cannot be said that the King James Version had enjoyed an auspicious launch. In fact, its appearance was something of an anticlimax.

CHAPTER 6

THE LIVELY ORACLES
OF GOD

Writing a century after the publication of the King James Version, Jonathan Swift lauded its creators:

> *The translators of our Bible were masters of an English*
> *style much fitter for that work than any which we see*
> *in our present writings, which I take to be owing to the*
> *simplicity that runs through the whole.*[1]

The point was well made. Like the mills of God, Bancroft's committee process did grind "slowly but exceeding small". His colleagues had the advantage that much of the milling had been done by other scholars over the previous half-century. Every word, every nuance of every word, and the doctrine depending on every word had been pored over and argued over. The Jacobean translators, therefore, understood well the importance of clarity and simplicity. They came to their task with a cool, one might almost say clinical, attitude.

When, in 1947, J. B. Phillips published a free translation of the New Testament epistles entitled *Letters to Young Churches*, he tried in his preface to explain something of what it felt like to grapple with the texts set down by the first-century authors. "Again and again," he recalled, "the writer felt rather like an electrician rewiring an ancient house without being able to 'turn the mains off'."[2] When we read the Authorized Version it is difficult to imagine the Jacobean scholars owning up to the same reaction. They seem to have been well insulated! To change the metaphor, they were not painting a heart-stopping, vibrant, disturbing masterpiece à la Breughel or Grünewald. What came from their brushes had more in common with a serene Ruysdael landscape or a refined Van Dyck portrait.

What they were most conscious of creating was a book for use in worship, a book that would be read aloud to passive but, hopefully, attentive congregations. Therefore it had to be mellifluous, easy on the ear. The constant refining and re-refining resulted in a text which had most irregularities ironed out and that flowed smoothly. One result was a proliferation of little literary gems – phrases which have endeared themselves to generations of readers and listeners and have lodged themselves firmly in the language: "gird up thy loins"; "physician, heal thyself"; "it is easier for a camel to go through the eye of a needle than for a rich man to enter the kingdom of God"; "wars and rumours of wars"; "they shall beat their swords into ploughshares". The 1611 translation has furnished the lyrics for most of our great religious music: Orlando Gibbons's "This is the record of John", Handel's "For unto us a child is born", Mendelssohn's "Oh for the wings of a dove". The language of the Authorized Version was designed for regular worship, for repetitive ritual. It was intended to unite English church people, not only by removing the choice of variant versions, but also by lodging itself securely in the minds of illiterate and semi-literate congregations.

Because its intended place was within the liturgy the 1611 translation was a closer in spirit to the Old Testament than the New. The Law, the Prophets, the chronicles, the religious poetry, and the wisdom literature of the Hebrew scriptures were designed for recitation in the synagogue. The precious scrolls containing Jewish religious texts were, and still are, treated with great reverence. They have an iconic character of their own. Generations of Jewish boys learned their people's scriptures by heart. The rituals of Passover and other annual celebrations involved the repetition of much-loved passages. In the best bardic traditions stories were related with relished, colourful detail:

> *In the year that king Uzziah died I saw also the Lord sitting upon a throne, high and lifted up, and his train filled the temple. Above it stood the seraphims: each one had six wings; with twain he covered his face, and with twain he covered his feet, and with twain he did fly. (Isaiah 6:1–2)*

The Jewish writers used vivid imagery to describe the relationship of Israel and Israel's God and when they were not conjuring up pictures they used repetition and other literary devices to drive home their message:

> *Thus saith the Lord; For three transgressions of Judah, and for four, I will not turn away the punishment thereof... (Amos 2:4)*

> *To every thing there is a season, and a time to every purpose under heaven: A time to be born, and a time to die; a time to plant, and a time to pluck up that which is planted; A time to kill, and a time to heal; a time to break down, and a time to build up... (Ecclesiastes 3:1–3)*

> *[Wisdom's] ways are ways of pleasantness, and all her paths are peace. (Proverbs 3:17)*

The seventeenth-century scholars caught well the mood of the original. In several places they did a better job than the translators of the Geneva Bible. Small changes added colour and fluency. For example, the earlier translation rendered Isaiah 2:4 as "They shall break their swords into mattocks, and their spears into scythes; nation shall not lift up a sword against nation, neither shall they learn to fight any more." After its passage through the ever-finer sieve of the King James Version scholars the same passage emerged as "They shall beat the swords into plow-shares, and their spears into pruning hooks; nation shall not lift up sword against nation, neither shall they learn war any more."

The New Testament is a very different animal to the Old. It is written in *koine*, the rough-and-ready dialect Greek of the first century. This had a limited vocabulary and lacked the grace and refinement of Classical Greek. Certainly there were passages where rhetoric or poetry raised the literary bar – the famous paean of love in I Corinthians 13 is a case in point – but the purpose of the New Testament was, first and foremost, didactic. The Gospels, the letters, the Acts of the Apostles, and Revelation were written to inform, instruct, encourage, and to eradicate error. Good translation of these books needed to reflect their immediate, rough-hewn character. By homogenizing the biblical language the translators lessened the impact of some New Testament passages. For example, Jesus had a lot to say about money, which, one might hope, the wealthy career bishops on the translation team took to heart. Did they feel a little uncomfortable about the Gospel assertion "Ye cannot serve God and riches" (Matthew 6:24)? Was that why, unlike the Geneva Bible, they preferred to leave untranslated the Greek *mammonas*, derived from the Aramaic "mammon"? "Ye cannot serve God and mammon" certainly sounds more comfortably remote.

Puritan scholars made great play with the translators' somewhat relaxed discipline. They insisted that using different English words to translate the same word in the original language involved a loss of precision. For example, in Hebrews 1:11–12 the Greek *himation* is rendered as both "garment" and "vesture". This makes for a more stylistically eloquent reading but, in so doing, it fails to capture the mood of the original *koine*. Perhaps more serious was an opposite tendency. The translators, for instance, used the word "hell" to translate three distinct biblical words. *Sheol* is the Hebrew abode of the dead; *hades* is the Greek underworld; and *gehenna* implies continual punishment. They are certainly not synonymous terms and treating them as such obscured the teaching of Jesus and the epistle writers.

There are passages where we can discern the translators' prejudices towards contemporary issues elbowing their way into the new text. In Romans 14 Paul was dealing with the attitude to be adopted to Christians who had scruples over minor issues of conduct. A literal translation of the Greek of verse one reads, "Now the being weak in the faith receive not to judgments of thoughts." Clearly this needed unpacking to make sense in English. Tyndale had been anxious to keep as close as possible to the original but accepted that some addition to the text was necessary. His version read, "Him that is weak in faith, receive unto you, not in disputing and troubling his conscience." The emphasis is on sensitivity towards the "weaker brother". When Bancroft's men got their hands on it, there was a distinct shift of emphasis: "Him that is weak in the faith receive ye, but not to doubtful disputations." It is hard to believe they did not have in mind those pestilential Puritans, always quibbling about niceties of ecclesiastical dress and ceremonies.

Even in a passage such as 1 Corinthians 13:1–13, where the 1611 translation magnificently and memorably presents Paul's teaching on brotherly affection within the church, we can detect a flaw. All previous English translations had rendered the Greek *agape* as "love", that most basic and vital of emotions. Only the King James Version insists on using the Latinized word "charity" – "now abideth faith, hope, charity, these three; but the greatest of these is charity". Why? Elsewhere, Bancroft's men had translated *agape* as "love". Can we discern here another example of party bias? The Westminster II committee which worked on the epistles was under the leadership of William Barlow, a secure member of the ecclesiastical establishment well in favour at court, an anti-Puritan controversialist, and often chosen by the king to preach against Presbyterianism. Strict Calvinists urged the total depravity of man, who was incapable of love without the infusion of divine grace. Arminians claimed that human beings could of their own free will respond to divine grace and were not predestined to salvation or damnation. "Charity" was a word which fitted in far better with the concept of "good deeds" than the more spiritually demanding "love".

The King James Version stressed on its title page that it had been "with the former translations diligently compared and revised". The original intention may have been to improve on the Bishops' Bible but, as we have seen, its major debt was to the Geneva Bible and Tyndale. However, Bancroft's men did not only have the results of their predecessors' labours to work with. The study of ancient languages had come on by leaps and bounds since the Marian exiles had beavered away at their tasks in foreign cities. Men who had studied the ancient texts for decades with the aid of the *Antwerp Polyglot* had developed a feel for the Old Testament writings. Nor were they working in English isolation. French and Spanish scholars were also applying themselves to the ancient texts and cooperation within the international community of academics often surmounted denominational barriers. This made possible a host of subtle refinements. The very opening words of the Bible revealed this. The Geneva Bible's beginning runs:

> *In the beginning God created the heaven and the earth.*
> *And the earth was without form and void, and darkness*
> *was upon the deep, and the Spirit of God moved upon the*
> *waters.*

The Authorized Version restored two phrases which the earlier translators had regarded as superfluous:

> *In the beginning God created the heaven and the earth*
> *And the earth was without form, and void, and darkness*
> *was upon the face of the deep. And the Spirit of God*
> *moved upon the face of the waters.*

The added words make for greater accuracy. It was on the *surface* of the oceans that darkness brooded and the divine spirit was active. And it is also more poetic.

Limitations of the Translation

However, the use the translators made of available sources was not faultless. As we have seen, they took as their basic New Testament text an edition by Theodore Beza, Calvin's successor at Geneva. This book, known later as the Received Text or *Textus Receptus*, contained a late Greek manuscript with a Latin translation and was believed to be the most reliable text available. In fact it was marred by scribal errors, additions, and omissions which had accrued over the centuries. Beza was not sufficiently critical of his source. This is all the more surprising because he actually had in his possession a fifth-century Graeco-Latin codex which he had obtained from a monastery near Lyons. Known as the *Codex Bezae*, it differed in many places from the *Textus Receptus*. Its renderings of the four Gospels, Acts, and parts of II John indicated that it derived from a different early tradition and that it might have been used as a means of correcting the *Textus Receptus*. Beza, however, had in most cases preferred to rely more closely on the later version, which was wrapped in the authority of long western tradition.

Most differences were not of a drastic nature. The most substantial passages which appeared in the *Textus Receptus* but not in sources now considered more reliable are Mark 16:9–20, which recounts various post-resurrection appearances of Jesus which are verified by other Gospel passages, and John 8:9–20. The latter is the story of the woman taken in adultery and has no parallel in the other narratives. However, it is much in sympathy with incidents involving Jesus' dealings with women (for example, the Samaritan woman in John 4) and this may have influenced the translators. More serious is the wording of I John 5:7. The *Textus Receptus* has, "There are three that bear record in heaven, the Father, the Word and the Holy Ghost: and these three are one." Those words, very conveniently, provide proof of the doctrine of the Trinity and this must have influenced the medieval scribe who copied and translated them into Latin. More reliable versions read, "There are three witnesses: the Spirit, the water and the blood; and all three give the same testimony." The words relate to the baptism and death of Christ and the inspiration of the Holy Spirit as means by which God validated the person and work of Jesus. Erasmus had spotted the fraud and omitted it from his *Novum Instrumentum* (though protests from the Roman establishment forced him to reinsert it in a later edition – see above, pp. 134) and the Geneva Bible did not include it. Beza, however, reinstated it and he was followed by the Authorized Version translation. Thus Bancroft's men handed the deists and other critics who did not believe in the Holy Trinity a ready-primed gun with which to shoot holes in orthodox Christianity. If the church had to rely on fake evidence to prove one of its core doctrines, what trust could anyone place in the church or its scriptures? Beza had also allowed his own theological bias to colour his annotations of the Greek text. Thus in Acts 2:47 he advised rendering *tous sozomenous* (literally "the being saved ones") as "those who should be saved", which fitted well with the Calvinist doctrine of election. In 1581 Beza had donated "his" codex to Cambridge University. Yet, despite having this precious aid to work from, the translators appear to have made little use of it.

The King James Version was, thus, very far from being the last word on the translation of Scripture into the English vernacular. It was very much a book of its time – a magnificent achievement but not without its faults; a rendition of a timeless text but one coloured by the issues and controversies of the day. Any attempt to take it "out of history" and elevate it to a position above criticism and contradiction does no favours to either it or the religion of English-speaking Christians.

The motivation behind the new Bible made it a different kind of book to every other version that had preceded it. It is so important to grasp this that it is worthwhile briefly reminding ourselves of the journey the word of God had taken over the previous millennium and a half. It was in the second and third centuries BC that Jewish scholars rendered their sacred writings into Greek for the benefit of their co-religionists living outside the Holy Land. This "Septuagint" was the version of the Old Testament eagerly taken up by Christians throughout the Gentile world. Devout Jews could only see this as a blasphemous misuse of the Law and the Prophets, and the Septuagint was banned in their communities. It was replaced by the Masoretic Text, produced painstakingly by scholars over many centuries. The objective was to discover and preserve an authentic, standardized Hebrew version, perfect in every detail, and the end result (c. AD 900) was a remarkable piece of work. Meanwhile, by AD 100, all the New Testament scriptures had been written and were in circulation. Everywhere the new faith took root, the primary Christian writings were copied and translated. Within another hundred years there were thousands of texts in circulation in Hebrew, Greek, Latin, Syriac, Coptic, Georgian, Arabic, Ethiopic, Nubian, Sogdian, Persian, Armenian, and Gothic. Standardization was, initially, less important for the Christian world than for the Jews of the diaspora (the five million Jews living outside Palestine). It was not until the new religion had established itself throughout the Roman world that it became necessary to create a universally accepted New Testament. It was to this task that Jerome addressed himself and he completed the Vulgate (literally the "common" version) translation of both testaments around 405 into the language spoken throughout the Roman world. The basic motivation of all these versions was didactic. The faith – whether Jewish or Christian – had to be passed on in as accurate a form as possible in order to instruct converts and young people, to unite believers and to outlaw heresy.

For the greater part of a millennium the Latin West was, more or less, satisfied with its official translation, though there were few parts of Europe where vernacular texts were not produced during the later Middle Ages. The sixteenth-century translators – Tyndale, Coverdale, and the scholars who laboured in Geneva, Rheims, and Douai – were also thinking didactically. Uppermost in their minds was providing a text for private study, doctrinal propaganda, and sermon preparation. Bancroft's team had different priorities. Their version had to circumvent any interpretation that might tend towards separatism (thus "bishop" was often preferred to "elder" and "church" to "congregation"). The educational role of the Bible was, of course, important but "education" for the framers of the King James Version was tied up with preserving the doctrinal and institutional integrity of the Church of England. The revisers of all the previous English translations inevitably forced the language of Tyndale, Coverdale, *et al.* into a mould of their own devising.

Reception of the King James Version

The King James Version was a masterstroke in the schema of Jacobean church–state propaganda, a fact which makes it difficult to understand why it was not launched with a triumphant blaring of trumpets. At the coronation of Charles I in 1625 and in every subsequent crowning ceremony, a copy of the King James Bible has been placed in the hands of the new sovereign with the words "We present you with this Book, the most valuable thing this world affords. Here is wisdom; this is the royal Law; these are the lively Oracles of God." Later ages have come to revere what is commonly known as the Authorized Version. But, whatever posterity has made of it, the new Bible did not set the Jacobean world on fire. No promotional budget was made available to ensure that the book became a bestseller. The king certainly made no effort to push it – further evidence, if any were needed, that James's interest in the project had flagged. No royal injunction or act of Parliament ordered it to be set up in churches. For the first time an "official" Bible appeared without a representation of the reigning monarch on the title page, which simply declared that the new translation was "appointed to be read in churches". The printer may well have hoped that this ambiguous wording would signify to many parish priests that they were obliged to equip their lecterns with the King James Version as soon as possible but in reality the book had no more authority than the Bishops' Bible. It was not an "authorized version" in any meaningful sense of those words.

The new Bible crept almost apologetically onto the market. It was unable to shoulder aside its more popular rivals. The two most influential religious books in Jacobean England were the Geneva Bible and John Foxe's *Actes and Monuments of the Christian Religion* (commonly called the *"Book of Martyrs"*). The latter had been a runaway bestseller since 1563 and had gone through six editions. Elizabeth had ordered all cathedrals to buy a copy and many churches had also acquired it. Most of Foxe's book was given over to a catalogue of men and women who had died for their faith under Catholic regimes. These stories of heroism, defiance, and sacrifice were the equivalent of those legends of the saints which had thrilled medieval Christians. As for the Geneva Bible it remained the most popular version of Scripture for at least a generation after 1611 and went on being printed until 1644. It was used for private devotion and study and was the version most often quoted by preachers. For those who wanted to have their cake and eat it, editions of the King James Version were printed together with the Geneva Bible's marginal notes. Even Lancelot Andrewes made extensive use of the Geneva Bible when writing his sermons. Together these two works made up the foundation for England's self-identification as the leader of European Protestantism. For several years the new translation made very little impact. It is significant that, as far as we know, it attracted hardly any criticism. One exception was provided by a certain Hugh Broughton. This elderly rabbinical scholar (born 1549) had long campaigned for a revision of the Geneva Bible and had expected to be included in the king's translation team. He bombarded Bancroft and his colleagues with suggestions and objections and it comes as no surprise that he was dissatisfied with the committee's work. He castigated the translators as time-servers dedicated to their own careers rather than to the sacred text entrusted to them. In particular he accused them of relegating better renderings to the marginal notes. He would, he railed, rather be "rent by wild horses" than commend the new translation to churches. It was, he insisted, only fit for burning. The sad fact about this disappointed man is that his own translations from biblical texts reveal considerable talent for rendering Hebrew idioms into English. Bancroft's committee would have benefited from Broughton's inclusion. Be that as it may, apart from Broughton's diatribe, the king's Bible appears to have been greeted with thundering apathy.

Publishing and Printing the King James Version

Therefore, how the "Authorized Version" came to achieve the place it held for more than three centuries in the affections of the English-speaking peoples does require some explanation. We will consider this in detail in later chapters but what is clear is that initial impetus was provided by commercial and political considerations. Robert Barker used his monopoly to ensure that no other folio editions of the English Bible were published after 1611. This meant that, sooner or later, churches would have to acquire the new book for their lecterns. Some did so straight away. Others waited until their worn-out older versions needed replacing. Meanwhile Barker continued to issue the Geneva Bible in smaller formats for personal and family uses. He could not ignore public demand for the familiar version. It took the determined efforts of crown and mitre to kill off the Geneva Bible. In 1625 Charles I came to the throne. He was as theologically blinkered as his father but lacked James's political pragmatism. He appointed as archbishop of Canterbury William Laud, the man who, as bishop of Bath and Wells (1626–28) and London (1628–33), had already shown himself to be the greatest scourge of the Puritans. One of Laud's first acts was to forbid the printing of the Geneva Bible. For the moment, this only put money in the pockets of Dutch printers who entered the market with alacrity, rather as their forefathers had a century earlier. When king and archbishop realized this they imposed a ban on the importation of the Geneva Bible. Even so, it was 1644 before the last Geneva Bible rolled off a foreign press. The supremacy of the King James Version could ultimately only be ensured by state censorship.

The promoters of the new Bible were at great pains to convince potential buyers that it was *not* new. Smith's preface set out to allay any such suspicions: "Truly (good Christian Reader) we never thought from the beginning that we should need to make a new translation." This reassurance was necessary because the era was long passed when the Bible had been an exciting novelty. No longer was reading it attended by a frisson of danger and the risk of incurring the wrath of the authorities. It had become a part of the church's antique furniture. People were used to seeing it on the lectern, hearing it read to them and preached from. Some enjoyed the freedom of being able to read it privately or with their families without being challenged. They did not want it taken away and replaced by a new version and they probably resented the suggestion that it should be tinkered with.

Translators and printers set out to give their work an aura of staid respectability. The first editions were set out in a heavy black letter, a typeface which was already old-fashioned. And the language itself did not reflect early seventeenth-century idiomatic English. The champions of vernacular Scripture had always valued clarity more than elegance. Erasmus had insisted "Christ wants his mysteries published as openly as possible" and had envisaged a world in which farmers at the plough and weavers at the loom would recite Scripture to themselves. Luther had rendered the Bible into an up-to-date German that bordered in places on journalese. He insisted that the text should feel as though "it had been written only yesterday". Tyndale's English was muscular, even boisterous. The same motivation cannot be discerned among the makers of the King James Version. They opted, whenever possible, for what would be respectable, uncontroversial, "safe". Their language was dated before their book hit the marketplace.

The Authorized Bible and Shakespeare's plays are often regarded as the twin pillars of English "golden age" literature. In fact, the place of the two corpuses in the development of language could scarcely be more different. Written English was a relatively new phenomenon. It was like a butterfly emerging from the chrysalis or a flower from the bud – full of exciting promise. Writers could be inventive, could do new things with it. Shakespeare is, of course, the supreme example; he added hundreds of words to the language. Bancroft's scholars neither enjoyed nor wished to enjoy this heady freedom. Their use of the vernacular, though rich, drew upon the established vocabulary of printed books and they were also influenced by the syntax of the Hebrew and Greek originals. If they produced, as they certainly did, an end product that was mellifluous and well-balanced it was because they were concerned with how their Bible would *sound* in worship rather than what literary merit it might possess.

The aura of antiquity and permanence was emphasized by the physical appearance of the new version. The title page of the first edition, by the rather undistinguished Antwerp engraver Cornelius Bol (or Boel), has the appearance of monumental masonry. In architectural niches prominence is given to the figures of Moses and Aaron, representing the divine law and priesthood. The twelve apostles are gathered in the "architrave" and the four Gospel writers appear in the corners of the composition. Like the Geneva Bible the title page emphasizes that the new translation is "out of the original tongue and with the former translations diligently compared and revised". Unlike the Geneva Bible, the new book can also claim to have been set in hand "by His Majesty's special Commandment". An interesting feature is the inclusion of Catholic imagery. It is quite likely that Cornelius Bol was a Catholic and that he naturally incorporated images with which he was familiar. The apostles are shown with the traditional symbols of their martyrdom and, at the foot of the page, there is a drawing of a pelican in her piety (a heraldic device depicting a pelican feeding her young with her own blood), which Catholic convention employed to represent the sacrifice of Christ in the mass.

The layout of subsequent pages is elegant, lucid, decorative – and "obstinately and deliberately archaic".[3] Like the Geneva and Bishops' Bibles, the text is divided into verses and, now, punctuation was added to make for ease of public reading. The crisp text in Gothic script is set in two columns per page within lined borders. Marginalia (restricted to variant readings) appear in Roman type.

The Bible's 6,637 notes are all philological and devoid of partisan theology. The publishers soon realized that this "respectable" image did not appeal to all potential customers. If they were to oust their rival from the market they had to copy some of the Geneva Bible's virtues. As early as 1612, thirteen quarto and octavo editions were produced in Roman script. By the 1640s the use of Gothic type had been abandoned altogether.

This was the book enthusiastically embraced by champions of the Anglican establishment. They saw it as a Trojan horse, which, once pulled inside the strict Calvinist citadel, would attack incipient separatism and establish doctrinal and liturgical unity. "Left wing" churchmen, by contrast, regarded it as merely one version among many which they felt free to use in support of their own religious opinions. It remained to be seen who would prevail.

CHAPTER 7

A MASS OF STRANGE
DELIGHTS

It would be easy to characterize the world into which the King
James Version was launched as one of violently clashing cultures.
The bloody and dramatic events which marked the first half of
the seventeenth century provide abundant evidence of political
and religious conflict. Britain was not the only country caught up
in the dislocation of the times. On the continent what have been
called the "Wars of Religion" may be said to have lasted from the
St Bartholomew's Day Massacre (1572) to the Peace of Westphalia
(1648). Yet for much of the reign of James I (1603–25), the king's
two nations were at peace. The failure of the Gunpowder Plot in
1605, a desperate terrorist measure to overthrow what Catholics
saw as an oppressive and heretical regime, sealed the fate of this
religious minority for more than two centuries. Until the outbreak
of civil war in 1642 the British islands were spared armed conflict.

However, King James's realm could not remain immune to the clash of ideologies.

The greatest impact on the lives of ordinary people over the preceding two generations had been what the historian, Professor Duffy, calls the "stripping of the altars", the removal from churches and, in most cases, the destruction of painted and carved religious images. The reformers were determined to obliterate all traces of papistical superstition and to put in their place the sole repository of religious truth – the written word of God. Now the pulpit and the lectern took pride of place over the altar. Symbol and sacrament were downgraded. The only music permitted was the singing of psalms to simple tunes. Faith became interiorized. It could only be apprehended and nurtured by prayerful reflection on the Scriptures. Church interiors, bright with sunlight through plain glass falling on whitewashed walls, emphasized the cool rationalism of reformed religion. The changes affecting every parish church were enormous but most significant doctrinally was the placing of the "apparatus" for the administration of word and sacrament. The reformers had removed chancel screens and any fittings which made the east end of the church into a "priest space" separate from the nave, where the passive laity sat. Further to emphasize their anti-sacerdotalism they replaced stone altars with wooden tables, which were set lengthwise in the chancel. The "sacrifice of the mass" thus became the Lord's Supper. The incumbent was no longer a "priest" whose main function was sacramental but a "minister" whose priority was the preaching of the word. To emphasize this, church interiors were dominated by pulpits and lecterns.

By 1603 most people had embraced or accepted these changes. Most but not all. There were those who could not relate to the austere and cerebral reformed religion. They needed sensual stimuli. Nor was it just Roman Catholic recusants who could not be reconciled to the new ways. There was still, within the national church, a clash between the "Catholic" and "Protestant" world views. Some churchwardens dragged their heels over the process of "purifying" their buildings and there were parishioners who, a few years later, welcomed the "high church" backlash inaugurated by Archbishop William Laud. He encouraged the reinstallation of stained glass windows and other decorations which, as he believed, "beautified" worship. More importantly, he ordered churches to move communion tables back to the east end and rail them off, thus making the altar and not the pulpit the visual focus of the church. The see-saw of English religion had taken another tilt. Inevitably the changes provoked reaction:

> ... there is a new font erected, over which certain carved images and a cross are placed, and also our communion table removed out of its ancient accustomed place, and certain images placed over the rail which stands about the table, all which, as we conceive, tends much to the dishonour of God.[1]

So complained the worshippers at All Hallows, Barking, and they were far from being alone. In point of fact, it mattered little what the ordinary men and women in the pews thought. The prevailing style in religion was set by the king and his bishops. Their principal concerns, as we have already seen, were authority and unity.

In the early seventeenth century a new influence pervaded the Stuart court – the baroque. This exuberant movement in the arts was all the rage in European society. It rebelled against the classical precision of the late Renaissance. Karl Baedeker's nineteenth-century travel guide to central Italy defined the movement as possessing "an undoubted vigour in the disposition of detail, a feeling for vastness and pomp, together with an internal decoration which spared neither colour nor costly material to secure an effect of dazzling splendour".[2] Baroque painting, architecture, and music were of the heart rather than the head, stronger on emotion than rationality.

It was in the year after the first publication of the King James Version that Thomas Howard, earl of Arundel began his career as a serious collector of art with a predilection for the voluptuous subjects, flowing curves, and radiant colours of the Venetian school. Howard (who would later introduce Rubens to England)

had a considerable influence on Prince Charles. Charles amassed
the largest collection of paintings ever assembled by an English
monarch. By 1620 an aesthetic clique had gathered around the
heir to the throne. To Puritan visitors this, coupled with costly and
elaborate masques and other court entertainments, was further
proof of the decadence of the ruling house. William Prynne was
the most outspoken critic of the Stuart court. In his *Histriomastix*
(1632) he denounced such frivolities as,

> *effeminate mixed dancing, stage plays, lascivious pictures,*
> *face painting, health drinking, long hair, love locks,*
> *periwigs, women's curling, powdering and cutting of their*
> *hair, bonfires, New Year's gifts, May games, amorous*
> *pastimes, lascivious effeminate music, excessive laughter,*
> *luxurious, disorderly Christmas-keeping, mummeries, with*
> *sundry suchlike vanities.*[3]

But it was not only such niggardly killjoys as Prynne who worried
about the gap opening between a closed, self-indulgent court and
the rest of the kingdom. Francis Bacon complained about royal
expenditure on costly "toys".[4]

But Puritans had a more fundamental objection to court style.
Unrestrained baroque exuberance smelled of Rome. In its reaction
to the Protestant revolt, the Counter-Reformation (the Catholic
campaign to purify the church) encouraged elaborate church decor
and ritual which made their appeal directly to the senses. It was easy
to make the connection between the mores of the royal household
and enmity towards England's Protestant identity. Both James
I and Charles I were married to Catholic princesses, who were
allowed (along with their attendants and friends) to enjoy Catholic
worship. Priests enjoyed protection at court and did not hesitate to
proselytize. The sight of the English *haut monde* indulging painted
and sculpted images, both sacred and profane, was an affront to the
Puritan conscience and made pious souls apprehensive about what
the future might bring. They were distrustful of the twin liturgical
pillars on which Anglican worship rested – the Prayer Book and

James I, attributed to John de Critz, the Elder (c. 1552–1642).

Richard Bancroft, the archbishop of Canterbury who headed the translation team. Artist unknown, after 1604.

Below: Portrait of a Young Puritan Boy, 1621 (oil on canvas). From an early age he would have been brought up to read the Bible.

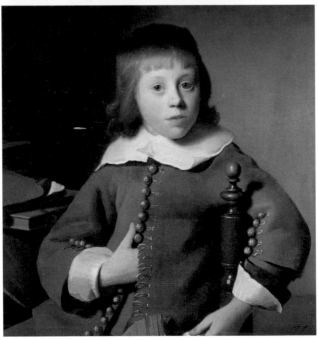

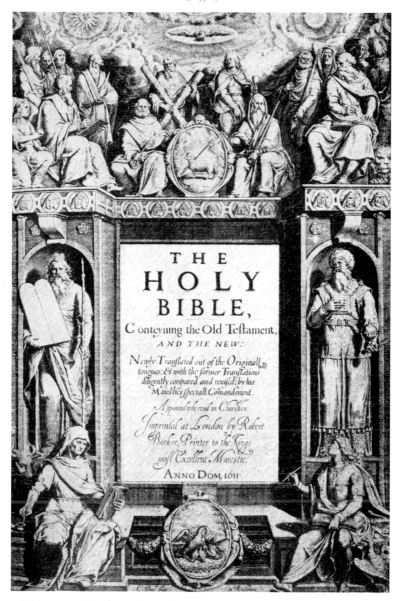

Title page of the first edition of the King James Bible, 1611, designed and
engraved by the Dutch master Cornelius Bol (or Boel), who has worked several
religious images into the design. The Hebrew letters for Yahweh, the dove,
and the lamb indicate the persons of the Trinity. The apostles are gathered
above with Matthew and Mark. Luke and John appear at the bottom. The title
is flanked by Moses and Aaron.

In *A Family Saying Grace Before the Meal*, an archetypal Calvinist family are depicted saying grace. Painted in 1585 by Anthuenis (Antoon) Claeissins or Claeissens (1536–1613).

Richard Mather (1596–1669): an early American woodcut, showing this founding father of the nation with his Bible.

William Hogarth's satirical take on 18th-century worship. While the parson prattles on oblivious of his hour glass, everyone else dozes off, including his clerk at the reading desk, on which stands the open Bible.

Victorian villagers from a fishing community make their way to church on a Sunday. Some carry Bibles.

For many the Bible was a treasured possession and was stored in its own, well-decorated container. This custom continued until the end of the 17th century.

The Chapel of Littlecote House, Berkshire, UK, showing the typical layout of a Puritan place of worship, with prominence given to the pulpit and reading desk.

"COMIC BIBLE" SKETCHES.—XVI.

JEHOVAH THROWING STONES.

"The Lord cast down great stones from heaven upon them unto Azekah, and they died."—Joshua x., 11.

By the late 19th century, atheists and critics of the Bible were becoming outspoken in their attacks on the text. This illustration from *The Freethinker* of March 1882 pokes fun at Joshua 10:11 by portraying the incident literally.

the Authorized Version. Before the reign ended, several ardent Puritans had taken their families across the Atlantic in search of a new homeland where they could practise "pure" religion.

The Impact of the King James Version on Society

For those who stayed devotional fervour became a contributory factor to politico-religious conflict. And it was Bible study and preaching which stirred devotional fervour. The seventeenth century was a golden age of preaching, particularly when compared with earlier times. Educational standards among the clergy were rising and, year on year, the number of non-preaching incumbents declined. This was due in part to the vigilance of bishops who made a point of hearing parish clergy preach during their visitations and several of whom called groups of ministers together for educational and training conferences. Such gatherings were similar to the "exercises" organized by Puritan enthusiasts in order to vet the style, content, and "soundness" of their colleagues. As well as Sunday sermons many people, particularly town-dwellers, had the opportunity to hear "lectures" or "prophesyings" delivered on weekdays. These were paid for by the bequests of godly philanthropists or from the common funds administered by urban councils. By no means was zealous preaching the preserve of religious radicals. High Anglicans were just as keen to indoctrinate their flocks against the "heresy" of Calvinist extremism. Whatever the motivation of the preachers or the doctrine they proclaimed, they all based their message on biblical texts. The approved method of presentation (certainly, but not exclusively, in Puritan circles) was, first, to expound the chosen verses in their context, then to expand on their teaching by cross-referencing to other Bible passages and, finally, to relate it to the lives of the hearers. Many of the best expositors published volumes of sermons or permitted their admirers to do so. Of Thomas Taylor, a minister at Reading in the 1620s and 1630s, it was said that he was a "walking Bible" and that he "maintained a little nursery of young preachers, who under his faithful ministry flourished in knowledge and piety".[5] To an extent never experienced before the people of England became familiar with the King James Bible. Its memorable phrases rang in their ears and lodged in their minds.

Not all preachers were poetic wordsmiths. Many of them, doubtless, wore down their hearers with lengthy, involved, text-overloaded expositions. It was far from unusual for a minister to preach for two hours on Sunday morning on an Old Testament text, two hours in the afternoon on a New Testament text, and then invite the congregation to assemble in the evening to discuss what they had learned. But some must have aspired to emulate the masters of their craft. Masters like John Donne, dean of St Paul's Cathedral, London, who in February 1630 preached his last sermon before Charles I and his court. His tour de force covered the entire Passion story:

> *From thence he was carried back to Jerusalem, first to Annas, then to Caiaphas, and (as late as it was) then he was examined and buffeted and delivered over to the custody of those officers from whom he received all those irrisions [mockeries] and violences, the covering of his face, the spitting upon his face, the blasphemies of words and smartness of blows, which that Gospel mentions; in which compass fell that crowing of the cock which called up Peter to his repentance. How thou passedst all that time last night, thou knowest. If thou didst anything then that needed Peter's tears, and hast not shed them, let me be thy cock. Do it now! Now thy Master (in the unworthiest of his servants) looks back upon thee. Do it now![6]*

Donne's contemporary George Herbert (1593–1633) was another upon whose soul the words of Scripture were indelibly printed and who, in his turn, turned them into poetry.

THE HOLY SCRIPTURES

Oh, Book! Infinite sweetness! Let my heart
  Suck every letter; and a honey gain,
  Precious for any grief in any part;

To clear the breast, to mollify all pain.

Thou art all health; health thriving till it make
  A full eternity. Thou art a mass
  Of strange delights, where we may wish and take.

Ladies, look here; this is the thankful glass

That mends the looker's eyes; this is the well
  That washes what it shows. Who can endear
  Thy praise too much? Thou art Heaven's lieger here,

Working against the states of Death and Hell.[7]

We could easily be persuaded by surviving sermons, tracts, and letters that the open Bible was transforming society from top to toe. There is, however, evidence that points towards a different conclusion. There were thousands upon thousands of ordinary men and women, especially in remoter areas, who seldom if ever went to church and had only the haziest of notions of what the Bible was all about.

At the beginning of the seventeenth century the rector of a
parish in Kent found that of four hundred communicants
"scarcely 40" had any knowledge about Christ, sin, death
and the afterlife. It was said of men in south Yorkshire
and Northumberland that they were totally ignorant of
the Bible and did not know the Lord's Prayer. A Yorkshire
boy when quizzed by a minister could not say "how many
gods there be, nor persons in the god-head, nor who made

the world nor anything about Jesus Christ, nor heaven or hell, or eternity after this life, nor for what end he came into the world, nor what condition he was born in". Otherwise he was "a witty boy and could talk of any worldly things skilfully enough". A Lancashire woman when asked about the Jesus Christ mentioned in the Creed, replied "she could not tell, but by our dear Lady it is sure some good thing, or it should never have been put in the Creed, but what it is I cannot tell you". An old man from Cartmel, also in Lancashire, a regular church attender, did not know how many gods there were. When Christ was mentioned by his questioner he said: "I think I heard of that man you spoke of, once in a play at Kendall, called Corpus Christi play, where there was a man on a tree, and blood ran down."[8]

Ignorance, illiteracy, and addiction to old superstitions were still formidable barriers to the realization of the Erasmus–Tyndale vision of every man his own Bible student. The Reformation's transformation of English Christianity from an image-based to a word-based religion was very far from being complete. The Bible – in whatever translation – remained a difficult book, even for those who could read, and preaching varied enormously in quality. We can have some sympathy with the 1624 parishioner who commented that when the minister went into the pulpit, she knew she was in for "such a deal of bibble-babble that I am weary to hear it and I can then sit down in my seat and take a good nap".[9] When we consider the influence of the Authorized Version throughout the seventeenth century (and beyond), we must keep at the back of our minds the large numbers of people who were not influenced by it at all, or, at least, only indirectly.

Throughout the thirty-one years between the publication of the King James Version and the outbreak of the Civil War churchgoers and ministers became increasingly accustomed to the officially approved text. With the passing of time it took on an aura of antiquity and it is probably this more than anything else which explains its gradually acquired dominance. Scholars were not oblivious to its defects and did not hesitate to publish new, corrected, editions. As early as 1616 the original publisher put out a folio copy with the more glaring errors corrected. A mere thirteen years later two members of the original Cambridge II team oversaw a complete revision (without the Apocrypha). Yet another – elegantly printed – Bible came from Cambridge in 1638. Some new editions and printings were just as prone to error as the original. Negatives appear to have posed particular problems for the publishers. A 1653 edition exhorted readers of Romans 6:13 not to "yield your members as instruments of righteousness" and prophesied that "the unrighteous shall inherit the kingdom of God" (I Corinthians 6:9).

The Geneva Bible continued to be a challenge in the personal study market. Cheap pocket and octavo editions were published and during the Civil War Scottish soldiers were buying knapsack copies for 1s 8d (about £7 in modern money). During the Commonwealth and Republic the printing monopoly was removed but this seems not to have resulted in a fresh flood of Geneva Bibles onto the market. What *did* happen was that the market came to be awash with pirate editions of the Authorized Version, many of them from foreign presses. This testifies to a growing demand, inspired to a considerable extent by large numbers of independent preachers and mountebanks who were taking advantage of the general anxiety and confusion (see below). Many of these cheap Bibles were rushed off the presses without such tiresome delaying formalities as proofreading. They therefore bristled with inaccuracies. Some had whole chunks of text missing. This brisk commercial activity is a good indication that the 1611 version had won general acceptance. When a triumphant Parliament abolished the Prayer Book, they did not also do away with the King James Bible.

Another pointer to the central position the King James Bible had already come to occupy was the use made of it by the major literary figures of the age. The political philosopher Thomas Hobbes wrote his seminal treatise on government – *Leviathan* – as a royalist in exile in France and his advocacy of absolutism did not go down well with parliamentarians. His response was that he based his argument on Scripture – an assertion he was able to support by drawing attention to the book's 657 biblical references. The two great literary giants of the Puritan scene generally preferred the Geneva Bible but were equally at home in the Authorized Version: Milton in *Paradise Lost* and Bunyan in *The Pilgrim's Progress* made reference to both versions.

The Bible in the Civil War

So, why did the 1611 Bible – so conservative, so staid, so uncontroversial – emerge triumphant from the turbulent years of the English Revolution? It was, I believe, precisely because those years were so turbulent. Turbulent and confused. During the appalling upheaval of 1642–48 army chaplains on both sides exhorted their troops from the same Authorized Version. This conflict was the bloody outcome of those politico-religious differences that had manifested themselves soon after the accession of James I. Parliamentary and royalist leaders claimed with equal fervour and sincerity the sanction of holy writ for their cause. We cannot read Oliver Cromwell's letters and speeches without acknowledging the formative influence the King James Version had on him. Not only did he quote from it frequently, his very language is coloured by it. Here he is addressing Parliament in September 1656, towards the end of his life.

> But I did read a Psalm yesterday; which truly may not unbecome both me to tell you of, and you to observe. It is the Eighty-fifth Psalm; it is very instructive and significant: and though I do but a little touch upon it, I desire your perusal at pleasure.
>
> It begins: "Lord, Thou hast been very favourable to Thy Land; Thou hast brought back the captivity of Jacob. Thou hast forgiven the iniquity of Thy People; Thou hast covered all their sin. Thou hast taken away all

*the fierceness of Thy wrath: Thou hast turned Thyself
from the fierceness of Thine anger. Turn us, O God of our
salvation, and cause Thine anger toward us to cease. Wilt
Thou be angry with us forever; wilt Thou draw out Thine
anger to all generations? Wilt Thou not revive us again,
that Thy People may rejoice in Thee?"...*

*Truly I wish that this Psalm, as it is written in the
Book, might be better written in our hearts. That we might
say as David, "Thou has done this," and "Thou has done
that;" "Thou hast pardoned our sins; Thou hast taken
away our iniquities!" Whither can we go to a better God?
For "He hath done it." It is to Him any Nation may come
in their extremity, for the taking away of His wrath. How
did He do it? "By pardoning their sins, by taking away
their iniquities!" If we can but cry unto Him, He will
"turn and take away our sins."*

*Then let us listen to Him. Then let us consult, and
meet in Parliament; and ask Him counsel, and hear what
He saith, "for He will speak peace unto His People."*[10]

Henry Vaughan (1622–95) was a royalist who fought on the side
of Charles I and hated most of what Cromwell and the Puritans
stood for. Yet he, like them, called for Bible-based simplicity. Here,
for example, is his reflection on the celebration of Christmas:

*The brightness of this day we owe
Not unto music, masque, nor show:
Nor gallant furniture, nor plate;
But to the manger's mean estate.
His life while here, as well as birth,
Was but a check to pomp and mirth;
And all man's greatness you may see
Condemned by His humility.
Then leave your open house and noise,
To welcome Him with holy joys,
And the poor shepherd's watchfulness:*

Whom light and hymns from heaven did bless.
What you abound with, cast abroad
To those that want, and ease your load.
Who empties thus, will bring more in;
But riot is both loss and sin.
Dress finely what comes not in sight,
And then you keep your Christmas right.

But it was not just the supporters of king and Parliament who turned to Scripture for solace and justification of their cause. The confusion of the times threw up a myriad of eccentric preachers with strange revelations to proclaim. Christopher Hill summarizes the age thus:

> *For a short time, ordinary people were freer from the*
> *authority of church and social superiors than they had*
> *ever been before… They speculated about the end of the*
> *world and the coming of the millennium; about the justice*
> *of God in condemning the mass of mankind to eternal*
> *torment for a sin which (if anyone) Adam committed;*
> *some of them became sceptical of the existence of hell.*
> *They contemplated the possibility that God might intend*
> *to save everybody, that something of God might be within*
> *each of us. They founded new sects to express these*
> *new ideas. Some considered the possibility that there*
> *might be no Creator God, only nature. They attacked*
> *the monopolization of knowledge within the privileged*
> *professions, divinity, law, medicine. They criticized the*
> *existing educational structure, especially the universities,*
> *and proposed a vast expansion of educational*
> *opportunity. They discussed the relation of the sexes, and*
> *questioned parts of the protestant ethic.* [11]

Liberty had become licence. Soldiers, artisans, tinkers, housewives took full advantage of their freedom to devise new ideas. They banded together in radical groups – Ranters, Diggers, Seekers,

Quakers, Fifth Monarchists, Levellers, Muggletonians. These were, as one contemporary complained, people "that would turn the world upside down, that make the nation full of tumults and uproars, that work all the disturbance in church and state… such men… should be suppressed… that we may have truth and peace and government again".[12] Every sect had its own revolutionary programme to propose for the reordering of society and every sect bolstered its arguments from Scripture – except the Ranters, who, allegedly, claimed that the Bible was the cause of all religious and civil discord and that "there would never be peace in the world till all the Bibles were burned".[13] This seemed to be the collapse of all order that Thomas More had prophesied over a hundred years before would follow from the Bible being available to all.

Parliament was well aware of the spread of this anarchy of ideas. In 1653 they debated the possibility of yet another revision of the sacred text to prevent the dissemination of eccentric versions by the wilder radicals. A committee set up to explore possibilities concluded that, while it contained some mistakes requiring correction, the King James Bible was recognized "to be the best of any translation in the world".[14] The Cromwellian regime had taken no action by the time the restoration of the monarchy put an end to such deliberation. Indeed, in 1656, Protector Cromwell further entrenched the King James Version by granting a monopoly to John Field (printer to Cambridge University) and Henry Hills, who, naturally, did all in their power to prevent the spread of rival versions. It is not to be wondered at that most of the subjects of Charles II, who came back to claim the crown in 1660, wanted above all things order, stability, and a return to what they thought of as "normality". The Bible produced under the aegis of Charles's grandfather and interpreted by duly appointed bishops and parish priests seemed to be the guarantor of a safe return to a mythical golden age.

The Bible after the Restoration

The politico-religious settlement of 1662, centred on the Act of Uniformity, seemed like the final triumph of Laudian high Anglicanism. Episcopacy was imposed upon the English and Scottish churches (Presbyterianism was restored in Scotland in 1689). Puritanism was outlawed. The kingdom had one national church. All congregations used a revised Prayer Book and the Authorized Bible. All? No, not quite. Almost 2,000 ministers and teachers who declined to be communicant members of the Church of England were deprived of their livelihoods. Most of them were university graduates and ministers of long experience whom the church could ill afford to lose, but such was the determination of the Restoration government to extract vengeance from those who had murdered the old king and humiliated the royalists in battle that those on the receiving end of the new legislation received no quarter. Some of the deprived ministers found employment as private chaplains or hospital chaplains. Others were reduced to doing manual labour or seeing their families starve.

But this brand of died-in-the-wool evangelicalism could not be crushed. The persecuted Nonconformists, as they now began to be called, took a leaf from the Catholics' book. Many of them met together in houses, barns, workshops, and the open fields to worship with the freedom they craved and to hear sermons from deprived ministers. Like the Catholics, they went in fear of informers and prosecution. Incidents like the following were common.

> *We were discovered by a malignant neighbour, who went*
> *and informed against us to the magistrates, who were then*
> *at feast with the mayor of the city. Three magistrates, with*
> *constables, and some of the baser and ruder sort, came*
> *to find us out and seize us. After they had searched an*
> *house or two, at length they discovered our little meeting,*
> *and found about twenty people, of whom three were aged*
> *ministers, and I the youngest of them. They gave us hard*
> *language, and treated us as if we had been the worst of*

> *malefactors. The ministers were committed to the care*
> *of the constables, to be by them sentenced to be sent to*
> *gaol, unless we would take the oath… We refused that*
> *oath… Then, they replied, "You must go to prison." I*
> *pleaded, that the Act did not extend to me, because the law*
> *expressly says: "That he must either be a Nonconformist*
> *turned out for Nonconformity, or one convicted of keeping*
> *Conventicles…" I had never had a benefice to be turned*
> *out of, neither was ever legally convicted of keeping*
> *Conventicles… yet they committed me to prison, without*
> *any law to warrant what they did.[15]*

Like Catholics, Nonconformists became adept at evading capture. Their version of the priest's hole was the hidden door or secret hatch in their meeting places by which ministers could escape.

Exactly what clandestine dissenters' worship consisted of is difficult to know. The evidence, for obvious reasons, is scanty but we can be certain that the sermon was its most important component. One report by a government investigator observed, "They never read a chapter in the Old or New Testament, nor so much as a verse, except it be for a proof in their teaching."[16] This should not be taken as an indication that the Bible had lost its importance for evangelicals; quite the contrary. Literate members of Nonconformist congregations had their own copies of the Scriptures and would often turn up the preacher's references as he spoke. On more than one occasion when government agents broke into a meeting, they discovered the minister fled and the people quietly reading their Bibles.

It has sometimes been suggested that oppressive Restoration legislation foisted two books on the British people – the revised Prayer Book and the King James Bible. This is not the case. There was no need to impose the Bible, because, as we have seen, it had by 1660 won general approval. Puritan and Nonconformist households were brought up on it in family prayers as well as Sunday worship. The Caroline divine, Jeremy Taylor, who had no sympathy with the radicals, published his devotional manual *Holy Living* ten years before the return of Charles Stuart. In it he advocated daily reading of the Scriptures as the most nourishing food for the Christian soul. It was not uncommon for those who took the Oath of Uniformity (the oath which enforced Anglican worship) to register their preference for the exposition of Scripture by turning up for Sunday worship when the liturgy had been completed and in time for the sermon. John Evelyn conscientiously recorded his record of church attendance in his *Diary* but it was always the sermons that he found worthy of note, for example:

> *3 November [1661] One Mr. Breton preached his*
> *probation sermon on I John 2.9, of God's free grace to*
> *penitents, etc; so as I could not but recommend him to the*
> *patron… 10 November Dr Paule preached coram Rege on*
> *II Pet. 2.20. Afternoon at the Abbey Dr Basiere… on I*
> *John 1.9 concerning the necessity of Confession; shewed*
> *that the Church of England was, for purity of doctrine,*
> *substance, decency and beauty the most perfect under*
> *heaven.[17]*

Sadly, Protestants who drew their inspiration from the same holy text were at odds and remained so for generations after the Restoration. It was persecution of Nonconformists that midwived the most Bible-drenched book in the English language, which was first published in 1678. John Bunyan (1628–88) wrote *The Pilgrim's Progress* during a spell of twelve years in prison for unlicensed preaching. "I was never out of the Bible, either by reading or meditation," he wrote when describing his own spiritual journey. That journey took allegorical form in *The Pilgrim's Progress*, a masterpiece which had more quotations per page from the King James Version than the most biblical sermon. For example, here is a passage describing the approach of Christian and Hopeful to their journey's end. They are met by Shining Ones, who describe the hilltop city before them:

> *There, said they, is "Mount Zion, the heavenly*

> *Jerusalem, the innumerable company of angels, and the*
> *spirits of just men made perfect." (Heb. xii.22–4) You*
> *are going now, said they, to the paradise of God, wherein*
> *you shall see the tree of life, and eat of the never-fading*
> *fruits thereof; and when you come there you shall have*
> *white robes given you, and your walk and talk shall be*
> *every day with the King, even all the days of eternity.*
> *(Rev. ii.7; iii.4, 5; xxii. 5.) There you shall not see again*
> *such things as you saw when you were in the lower region*
> *upon the earth – to wit, sorrow, sickness, affliction, and*
> *death: "for the former things are passed away." (Isa.*
> *lxv.16, 17.) … You must there receive the comforts of all*
> *your toil, and have joy for all your sorrow; you must reap*
> *what you have sown, even the fruit of all your prayers,*
> *and tears, and sufferings for the King by the way. (Gal,*
> *vi.7, 8.) In that place you must wear crowns of gold, and*
> *enjoy the perpetual sight and visions of the Holy One; for*
> *"there you shall see him as he is." (1 John iii.2.)*

Yet, again we have to recognize that devotion to the Authorized Version was not confined to those on the Protestant "left". It was Thomas Traherne (1637–74), a humble Anglican parish cleric (and one who lived in almost complete obscurity until his writings were discovered in the nineteenth century) who described how his imagination was fired by the sacred text:

> *I can visit Noah in his ark, and swim upon the waters of*
> *the deluge. I can see Moses with his rod, and the children*
> *of Israel passing through the sea… I can visit Solomon*
> *in his glory, and go into his temple, and view the sitting*
> *of his servants, and admire the magnificence and glory of*
> *his kingdom. No creature but one like the Holy Angels can*
> *see into all ages… It is not by going with the feet, but by*
> *journeys of the Soul, that we travel thither.*[18]

So committed was Traherne to the Bible and its exposition that he asked to be buried in his church at Teddington "under the reading desk".

Traherne was too young to be involved in the Civil Wars, though he ended his days as chaplain to Sir Orlando Bridgeman, the judge who presided at the trial of the regicides, the men who had signed Charles I's death warrant.

As this troubled century drew to its close it was the poet John Dryden (1631–1700) who, seeking the source of religious authority, found it in the Bible:

> *Then for style, majestic and divine*
> *It speaks no less than God in every line.*

In his poem *Religio Laici* of 1682 he urged that everyone capable of doing so should study the sacred text:

> *The unlettered Christian who believes in gross [in*
> *generalities],*
> *Plods on to heaven and ne'er is at a loss…*
> *The few by Nature formed, with learning fraught,*
> *Born to instruct, as others to be taught,*
> *Must study well the sacred page, and see*
> *Which doctrine, this or that, does best agree*
> *With the whole tenor of the work divine,*
> *And plainliest points to Heaven's revealed design.*

Dryden was contending against deism, currently fashionable in intellectual circles, which proposed faith in a supreme being who could be apprehended only by reason and reflection on the works of nature. The poet, while accepting that the Bible had its errors and inconsistencies, asserted that it was still God's self-revelation and was, therefore, the only guide for men to live by. And what Dryden meant by the Bible was the King James Version.

By the last quarter of the seventeenth century this text had come into its own as the undisputed narrative of God's story for English-speaking peoples.

Chapter 8

Travels and Travails

When Charles II's subjects looked back across the political upheavals of the mid-seventeenth century it was almost inevitable that they should envisage antediluvian England as a land of blessed peace, concord, and artistic achievement. It was the fashionable society presided over by Charles II that rediscovered Shakespeare, Jonson, and their contemporaries. The London theatre thrived as never before and many Jacobean masterpieces were revived. It was in this atmosphere that the King James Version emerged finally as the unchallenged English Bible, glowing with an aura of antiquity and respectability. It became a potent symbol of "Englishness". The spirit of the age is epitomized in the career of Nahum Tate (1652–1715). This son of a Puritan divine established himself among the literati of late Stuart London as a poet and dramatist. He gained a fashionable following with "improved" versions of Shakespeare's plays – including an adaptation of *King*

Lear with a happy ending! But he also turned his attention to the book of Psalms and, with Nicholas Brady, produced new metrical settings for public worship. It was now that the Bible came to be set alongside the corpus of Shakespeare and regarded as one of the twin pillars of English literature. Only half a century separated the death of Shakespeare (1616) from the heyday of Milton, Dryden, and Bunyan. Restoration cognoscenti could venerate the Bible as a literary gem without having to negotiate linguistic hurdles in their efforts to get to grips with the sacred text.

However, the Bible was not and is not an easy book to understand. The compendious glosses of the Geneva Bible had been included largely for reasons of religious polemic but they were also there to illuminate the more obscure passages. Various editions had also been supplied with maps, charts, timelines, and other illustrations for the help of students. Such embellishments had been strictly outlawed from the King James Version, which, as we have seen, was not designed primarily for personal use. It was left to concerned teachers and pastors to provide aids to study.

One such was the "paraphrase", which avoided copyright complications by not quoting the 1611 directly. Such publications contained portions of the text interspersed with explanatory notes. Henry Hammond, one of the most engaging characters of the troubled mid-seventeenth century, suffered imprisonment and deprivation of his living because of his royalist sympathies but he was respected on both sides of the political divide for his profound learning and benevolence. His *Paraphrase and Annotations of the New Testament* (1653) earned Hammond recognition as the father of English biblical criticism. A writer of very different character was Daniel Whitby (1638–1726), a born controversialist who seems to have been unable to encounter an argument without joining in. His written works included attacks on Catholics and Calvinists but his *Paraphrase and Commentary on the New Testament* (1702) was widely valued and continued in print until 1822.

These and other study aids had apologetic as well as devotional uses. The King James Version was fully available to the Bible's enemies as well as its friends. In the new rational spirit of the times critics inevitably pointed out apparent inconsistencies and implausibilities in the Bible. Just as the medieval hierarchy had insisted that only the church could interpret Scripture and guard against heresy, so leaders of the British churches believed the King James Version needed defending from the cohorts of rationalism. "Harmonies" were produced. These were Gospel passages rearranged to form a continuous narrative. Such "scissors and paste" jobs were intended to eradicate seeming contradictions between the accounts of the evangelists. For example, James Macknight in his *Harmony of the Four Gospels* (1756) extended Jesus' ministry by treating several parallel passages as though they referred to separate incidents.

Throughout the eighteenth century there was a widening gulf between the educated minority whose culture was to a large degree shaped by the English Bible and the unlettered majority who were as distant as ever from the church. Many Christian leaders and pastors, painfully aware of this fact, were dissatisfied with the King James Version and scarcely a decade passed without new works of consequence being published to help Christians in their reading and understanding of Scriptures. Daniel Mace (d. 1753) wanted to give the Bible more "punch" and used idiomatic English. It was a sound instinct; the 1611 version was by now sounding very antiquated, its Latinisms particularly standing out from the common speech of the people. For example, in Romans 6:14, the Authorized Version exhorted people not to let sin "have dominion over" them. Mace preferred the more direct "lord it over". The 1611 version was also cautious in matters of delicacy. There is no doubt that in 1 Corinthians 7:36, where Paul is advising young people how to handle sexual passion, the Authorized Version left something to be desired: "If any man think that he behaveth himself uncomely toward his virgin." However, Mace's rendering was perhaps a little too "cool": "If any man thinks it would be a reflexion on his manhood to be a stale bachelor."[1]

Edward Harwood (1729–94) erred in the opposite direction in *A Liberal Translation of the New Testament; Being an Attempt to translate the Sacred Writings with the same Freedom, Spirit and Elegance with which other English Translations from the Greek Classics have lately been executed* (1768). It aimed at a dignified rendering of the sacred text. The result was often humorous banality. Thus, Peter, overawed by the transfiguration (Luke 9:33), responds, "Oh, Sir! What a delectable residence we might establish here!"

In 1755 no less a personage than John Wesley (1703–91), who knew better than most men the problems of conveying biblical truth to illiterate and semi-literate crowds and who was eager to equip Methodist preachers with the tools to continue his evangelistic enterprise, produced a revision of the King James New Testament. It was written, as he said, "for plain, unlettered men who understand only their Mother Tongue". It was a conscientious work based on the best available Greek texts. But, perhaps more importantly, it breathed the conviction and immediacy that had fired the original writers and which were captured in the Evangelical Revival. Yet, despite all these endeavours, nothing could dislodge the 1611 Bible from its place in the British church.

The Bible in America

Another reason for the success of the Authorized Version was the migration of English people – and therefore their language and religion – from their native shores. The second half of the seventeenth century witnessed an explosion of interest in the New World. Hundreds of bands of settlers, following the example of the Pilgrim Fathers in 1620, made for the eastern American seaboard and the Caribbean. Many, but not all, were fleeing from a land where they believed they were not free to worship and develop their spiritual lives as they wished. Naturally, they took their Bibles with them. We might have expected that they would replicate in their new homeland the usage of various translations existing in the mother country, with the preference being for the Geneva Bible. In fact the political development of the colonies actually led to the enthroning of the Authorized Version. Colonial governors were very wary of the threat of anarchy in their territories as various groups of settlers and their charismatic leaders set up their own communities. Pastors and magistrates worked together to maintain as much unity as possible and it was, ironically, the King James Version that became the staple source for religious preaching and teaching. At the same time, economic considerations inhibited any temptation that might have existed to make variant texts available or even to create an "American Bible". The colonists lacked the large presses and supplies of paper that would have been necessary for the printing of Bibles in the New World. They were, thus, totally dependent on imports from Britain. As long as relations with the mother country remained on an even keel, there was no problem. But with the passage of time the interests of the two sides inevitably diverged. In 1774 the separate colonies came together in the first Continental Congress to make a united stand against what they considered to be British exploitation. One of the first decisions the Congress took (1775) was to ban the import of British goods – and that included Bibles.

Over the next few years, then, while the United States of America was going through painful birth pangs, pastors, teachers, and worshippers suffered an increasing shortage of Bibles. Congress received a petition from leading clergy "that under your care and by your encouragement, a copy of the holy Bible may be printed, so as to be sold nearly as cheap as the common Bibles, formerly imported from Britain and Ireland".[2] Unfortunately, the government of newly independent USA showed itself no more eager to put its hand in its pocket than had the government of James I. It was left to private enterprise to make good the deficiency.

The first to clamber into the breach was the Philadelphia Scotsman Robert Aitken. He published a King James Version New Testament in 1777. Four years later he persuaded Congress to support his printing of the whole Bible. But not with money. The states' representatives would not even authorize the book for distribution. Not until Aitken had invested some £3,000 of borrowed capital did the government mildly "recommend this edition of the Bible to the inhabitants of the United States". Poor Aitken went bankrupt.

But he had blazed the trail. The undeniable demand for Scripture and the fact that publishers in the USA were free from all copyright restrictions meant that publishers with deeper pockets or more business acumen than Aitken could produce new editions. In 1791 Isaac Collins made the first folio edition designed for family reading and Isaiah Thomas produced an illustrated Bible. It was the King James Version the pioneers took with them as they moved inexorably westwards through the vast spaces of the Midwest. In 1816 the American Bible Society came into being, an interdenominational body dedicated to meeting the challenges of westward expansion and immigration by providing a standard English text which would give the growing nation a firm base for its moral and religious principles.

The rapid expansion of the USA presented a massive and complex missionary challenge to the Christian churches. Immigrants were arriving by the tens of thousands every year from many different countries. They needed the Scriptures in their own languages but, at the same time, they needed to be integrated into the Christian culture of the USA. As they and, more particularly, their children developed fluency in the English language, they were deeply influenced by the King James Bible. We might wonder how Russians, Poles, Italians, Germans, and other new arrivals coped with the antiquated text of the Authorized Version. The answer is that nineteenth-century American English was closer to the language spoken in Britain two hundred years earlier than the English then being spoken in the old mother country. Vocabulary, grammar, and style had changed slowly in the colonies. When an immigrant read in Job 28:15 "Wisdom... can not be gotten for gold" the words did not strike him or her as antiquated. The phrasing and cadences of the King James Version permeated the written language of educated Americans. For example, J. T. Trowbridge in the late 1860s observed about post-Civil-War society, "There is at this day more prejudice against color among the middle and poorer classes who owned few or no slaves than among the planters who owned them by the hundred."[3] The writer was, doubtless unconsciously, echoing the phraseology of Luke 15:7: "Joy shall be in heaven over one sinner that repenteth, more than over ninety and nine just persons, which need no repentance." And when we consider American political oratory we cannot but be struck by its biblical tone. On 4 March 1865 Abraham Lincoln made his second inaugural address to Congress and his words have entered the nation's folklore:

> ... *With malice toward none; with charity for all; with firmness in the right, as God gives us to see the right, let us strive on to finish the work we are in; to bind up the nation's wounds; to care for him who shall have borne the battle, and for his widow, and his orphan – to do all which may achieve and cherish a just and lasting peace among ourselves, and with all nations.*[4]

It was not just the sentiment that was biblical. To this day American political oratory uniquely owes an obvious debt to the King James Bible.

The American Bible Society did not only have the needs of newcomers in mind. As the settlers moved westwards they encountered Amerindian tribes who had hitherto had no contact with the white man. These "savages" needed evangelizing and the Bible-toting "preacher-man" became a stock figure on the frontier, a buffer between the rival interests of indigene and incomer and someone destined to be parodied in twentieth-century Hollywood epics. By the mid-nineteenth century the American Bible Society had distributed over five million Bibles or New Testaments, and had placed copies in schools, prisons, naval vessels, and military barracks. During the Civil War (1861–65) 1.5 million copies of the King James Version were given to Unionist soldiers and 300,000 to Confederate troops.

By this time the American Bible Society had joined its British counterpart in translating the Scriptures into the languages of the wider world. The British and Foreign Bible Society had only come into being in 1804 but its foundation was one step in a process that had been going on for more than a century.

The Bible in the British Empire

The USA might have been lost to Britain but imperial expansion was, by this time, well under way elsewhere. The planting of trading posts throughout the Orient, territory-grabbing in India, the opening up of areas for white settlement in Canada, Australia, and New Zealand led to the establishment of "expat" communities which transplanted British culture into foreign soils. That included the building of churches, the replication of Anglican and Nonconformist worship, and the public reading of the King James Version. Many Protestant merchants, administrators, and military officers had taken seriously Jesus' commission to "teach all nations" (Matthew 28:19) as they laboured in "heathen lands afar" but there was little enthusiasm among the ecclesiastical establishment for properly organized missionary work. The pioneer Thomas Bray (1656–1730) carried on for many years a one-man campaign to provide ministers and books for locations in colonial outposts. This led to the founding of the Society for the Propagation of Christian Knowledge (1699) and the Society for the Propagation of the Gospel in Foreign Parts (1701). Yet it was another hundred years before organized proselytizing endeavour really got under way with the foundation of missionary societies by the mainstream churches. However, when the movement did get going, it turned into a veritable crusade active throughout the nineteenth and much of the twentieth centuries. It was to serve the missionaries that the British and Foreign Bible Society (now the Bible Society) came into being in 1804. Its objective was to provide vernacular Bibles for use wherever the missionaries were working. When, in the second half of the century, the USA embarked upon its own career of commercial and colonial expansion, the American Bible Society took on a similar role. The work of the Bible Society is only tangential to the story of the King James Version but it was part of the emphasis on education and literacy that is very pertinent to our theme. Protestant missionaries viewed the setting up of schools and colleges as a vital part of their civilizing activity. Throughout Asia, Africa, and the Americas there grew up a literate indigenous elite from which would come, in due course, the rulers, administrators, lawyers, and clergy of independent nations. As they learned the language of their colonial masters, they inevitably studied and had their thought forms moulded by the King James Version.

Ironically, while the King James Version was being received throughout the British empire as a hallowed text, above contradiction, and resistant to change, in Britain itself it was facing many challenges. The eighteenth century was one of interlinking revolutions. The Enlightenment infused severe rationalism into philosophical and religious thought. Social upheaval, in part impelled by new egalitarian principles, convulsed several European countries. Industrial revolution created factory towns inhabited by a new class of urban poor. In this atmosphere the accepted Bible text was confronted by enemies who rejected its teaching but it also experienced pressure from friends: biblical scholars who wanted to make it more accurate, cultural gurus who wanted to improve its language, and zealous preachers and teachers who wanted to make it more relevant.

By the mid-eighteenth century it was not possible to speak of *the* King James Version because several variant printings were in existence. The number of linguistic and typographical errors amounted to a virtual scandal. Part of the problem arose from the onward march of scholarship. As scholarly techniques improved and as new manuscript discoveries were made, the shortcomings of existing versions became more obvious. The King James Version had not been on sale for sixteen years before another early Greek text had become available in England. In 1627 a text of the Bible older than anything hitherto known in England suddenly made its appearance. The *Codex Alexandrinus*, an early fifth-century document, was presented to Charles I by the Orthodox patriarch of Constantinople. Its four volumes and 773 vellum pages contained most of the canonical books plus the non-canonical I and II Clement. Yet still there was no official move to update the King James Version. No archbishop or king or senior theologian made any such proposal. The prospect of embarking on another seven-year translation project could not be entertained.

Not until the mid-eighteenth century was a serious attempt made to create a standard, accurate text. Scholars at both Oxford and Cambridge set their minds to the task but it was the revision produced by Dr Benjamin Blayney (later Regius Professor of Hebrew) of Hertford College, Oxford in 1769 which proved to be the more thorough piece of work. Blayney made 24,000 corrections to the 1611 text. This version, known commonly as the Standard Text, has remained the basis for almost every edition published since 1769. At last the English-speaking Protestant world had a Bible which commanded general support. It soon had the means to produce large quantities of books at modest prices. The Industrial Revolution resulted in a sequence of improvements in the printing process, culminating in the first steam-powered press (1814). An accurate text, cheap copies, an ever-growing international market – publishers of the King James Version now had all the ingredients necessary for success.

The nineteenth century was the apogee of Anglo-Saxon world domination. Britain and its empire, the USA, and its satellites enjoyed cultural and economic influence over much of the world's surface. At the end of that century a writer on English literature could assert without fear of contradiction,

> … *the English Bible is the chief bond which holds united in a common loyalty and a common endeavour, the various branches of the English race. The influence of the Bible can be traced through the whole course of English literature and English civilisation, and, more than anything else, it tends to give unity and perpetuity to both.*[5]

By the English Bible the author, of course, meant the King James Version.

The Growing Popularity of the King James Version

The nineteenth century was certainly the epoch of its greatest triumph. The cultural leaders of the age sang its praises. John Ruskin (1819–1900) described it as "the most precious, and, on the whole, the one *essential* part of all my education". Lord Macaulay (1800–59) regarded it as "a book which, if anything else in our language should perish, would alone suffice to show the whole extent of its beauty and power". Even Thomas Huxley (1825–95), the stalwart champion of Darwin's *Origin of Species*, scourge of organized religion and, on his own confession, the first "agnostic", observed (perhaps with some exaggeration),

> ... *for three centuries, this book has been woven into the life of all that is best and noblest in English history...*
> *it has become the national epic of Britain, and is familiar to noble and simple, from John o'Groat's House to Land's End, as Dante and Tasso once were to the Italians... it is written in the noblest and purest English, and abounds in exquisite beauties of pure literary form...* [6]

On the other side of the Atlantic it was said of Abraham Lincoln (1809–65) that he

> *built up his entire reading upon his early study of the Bible. He... mastered it absolutely; mastered it as later he mastered only one or two other books... mastered it so that he became almost "a man of one book".* [7]

But if this was the period when the King James Version was at its most secure, it was also the age which saw it facing its most serious criticism. The challenges came from the scientific community, liberal trends in biblical criticism, and fresh documentary evidence. Nor had it shaken off the terrier-like attacks of those who still wanted to see the word of God made available in more accessible and "modern" translations.

In the power structures of the British church there had occurred something of a *volte-face* since the days of Stuart rule. The heirs of the Puritans – the evangelicals – had become the dominant, or, at least, the most vigorous party. As the historian G. M. Young observed,

> *Evangelicalism had imposed on society, even on classes which were indifferent to its religious basis and unaffected by its economic appeal, its code of Sabbath observance, responsibility, and philanthropy; of discipline in the home, regularity in affairs; it had created a most effective technique of agitation, of private persuasion and social persecution.*[8]

In both Britain and the USA revivalism, which had manifested itself in the work of John Wesley and Jonathan Edwards in the eighteenth century, reappeared in "waves" right up to 1914. Preaching for conversion is associated with such men as the American Charles Grandison Finney (1792–1875) and Dwight L. Moody (1837–99) and the British Thomas Chalmers (1780–1847) and William Booth (1829–1912). Finney, minister of the Broadway Tabernacle, presided for many years over a growing church in the centre of New York and wrote a book on the technique of revivalism, which was hugely influential on both sides of the Atlantic. Moody is best remembered in Britain for the evangelistic campaigns he led with his hymn-writing friend, Ira D. Sankey, in the 1870s and 1880s but he had already spent years working in the slums of Chicago. Chalmers was one of the great pulpit orators of the day and made a great impact on political leaders such as William Wilberforce. William Booth is, of course, well known as a tireless preacher and social worker in the slums of London and as the founder of the Salvation Army. These were just some of the great evangelistic luminaries of the day. There were numerous other earnest lay and ordained, Bible-based men and women working in the "home mission". They have left a permanent mark on the landscape in the shape of nineteenth-century churches, chapels, daughter churches, and mission halls – and an even deeper impression on the national psyche. They were prominent in every area of social improvement, from the abolition of slavery to prison reform, from elementary education to factory legislation. And their motivation was to be found in the Bible. They were not, of course, the only philanthropic activists nor the only people who held the Authorized Version dear but they were the people who set the tone of society. Historian D. W. Bebbington rightly claimed, "The hundred years or so before the First World War... deserve to be called the Evangelical Century."[9] It was evangelicals who took the lead in elevating the King James Version to a prominence it had never enjoyed before. The lord lieutenant of one of the English shires reminisced that there were only two of his acquaintances among the leaders of county society who did not lead their households in family prayers.

Like their Puritan predecessors, evangelicals were to the fore in the campaign for education. If converts were to grow in the faith, it was essential that they should be able to read the Bible. More than that, the word of God was an infallible moral guide for all. By the early years of the nineteenth century it is probable that at least fifty per cent of British adults were literate. But that meant that about fifty per cent were not – most of them, of course, in the lower strata of society. It was the churches which led the campaign to address this situation. The work of the voluntary section embraced Sunday schools, ragged schools for the children of the urban poor, night schools for working men, and other initiatives. Churches also sponsored the foundation of elementary schools and there developed a rivalry (not always healthy) between the Anglican National Society for Educating the Poor in the Principles of the Established Church and the Nonconformist British and Foreign School Society. The obvious merit of these charitable societies prompted government action. The Education Act of 1870 introduced state education by providing schools for children under thirteen funded from the rates in places where the denominational societies were not active. Needless to say, study of the Bible (usually involving rote-learning) occupied an important place in the curricula.

Physical proof of the influence of the Authorized Version is to be found in the numerous editions of the 1769 text which poured from the presses. There were family Bibles – impressive tomes with spaces provided for the pasting-in of family trees and photographs. There were study Bibles with extensive footnotes and interleaved commentaries. There were illustrated Bibles containing not only maps, charts, and engravings of the flora and fauna of the Holy Land, but also engravings after Old Master paintings from the Renaissance masters to the Victorian realists. This was the era of the scrapbook. Men and, more particularly, women kept elaborate albums in which to keep poems, original artwork, and steel and lithographic engravings. People, most of whom were never likely to leave their native shores, were fascinated by the tales of foreign lands brought back by missionaries, explorers, and travellers. They read books and accounts in the missionary journals; they attended lantern-slide shows and they collected cheap prints. Their Bibles reflected these trends.

One of the more remarkable men who played a bit part in the drama of the King James Version was John Kitto. It would be difficult to imagine a less likely participant. Kitto was born in 1804, the illegitimate son of a Cornish stonemason. He was very small (less than 1.5 metres) and far from robust, scarcely the sort of child who could follow his father's trade. However, when he was ten, what little schooling he had came to an abrupt end and he had to assist in the family business. He was only twelve when he fell from a ladder while carrying a load of heavy slates. He survived but the accident left him totally deaf. His father could not afford to feed an unproductive son and John was sent to the workhouse. There, like many others, he might have ended his days – sooner rather than later. What saved him was his obsession with books. Kitto was a compulsive student and his intelligence was recognized by some of the local gentry. One of them was Anthony Norris Groves, a founder member of the evangelical sect of Plymouth Brethren. As a result of chapel preaching and the kindness shown him by

Groves's family he underwent a conversion experience.

Groves recognized the young man's literary potential. Kitto had a vigorous and fluent writing style and a keen eye for detail. His patron took him on a missionary journey to the Middle East and Kitto wrote an account of their exciting travels which involved flood, an outbreak of plague, and a military siege. This was a time when English readers were hungry for knowledge of foreign lands and, on his return, Kitto found himself much in demand as a writer of magazine articles and entries for the publications of the Society for the Diffusion of Useful Knowledge.

In 1834 his gifts were recognized by another patron, a typical representative of the nineteenth century's passion for knowledge. Charles Knight was a publisher and magazine editor. One of the projects he employed Kitto for was the *Pictorial Bible*. This appeared first of all in monthly instalments and was then reissued in bound editions. The objective was to encourage people to read the Authorized Version by illustrating the text with hundreds of engravings, largely after Old Master originals. This was a return to the technique used by Tyndale and Coverdale, the first translators into English. Following the success of this project, Kitto produced for Knight an illustrated Bible commentary in five volumes.

Kitto's prodigious energy and his need for money (he had married in 1833 and sired a large family, seven of whom survived into adulthood) drove him on to other ambitious projects. He never achieved the kind of remuneration his industry deserved but the literary establishment recognized his worth. Remarkably, by the time of his death in 1854, John Kitto had been made a fellow of the Society of Antiquaries, had received an honorary doctorate from the University of Geissen, and had been awarded a government pension of £100.

The strangest accolade of all was *Kitto's Bible*. This was produced by a London print seller, John Gibbs, who decided to expand Kitto's *Pictorial Bible*. He interleaved with the original text 30,000 additional drawings and prints and hundreds of illustrations taken from other Bibles. The result was sixty-six large folio volumes in which scarcely a single incident, building, landscape, and personality was not represented pictorially. This curio is now housed in the USA's Huntington Library. It is a pity that Kitto's name should be remembered by being linked with such a useless oddity. His life is a more fitting testament to his self-imposed mission to make the Bible better known. He died at the age of forty-nine worn out by his ceaseless labours.

But while the King James Version was being so monumentally celebrated, its inadequacies were being pointed out by others no less devoted to the propagation of the divine message.

CHAPTER 9

PROGRESS OR
PROFANITY

In scholarly circles there was mounting concern about the inaccuracy of the King James Version. European expansion and imperial rivalry led to growing involvement by western powers in the lands of the Bible. Napoleon briefly conquered Egypt (then part of the Turkish Ottoman Empire) in 1798–1800 and, though the Turks regained nominal control of territory which extended around most of the Mediterranean littoral, they were increasingly under European influence. One result was that archaeologists, historians, and linguists frequently visited the Levant gaining fresh knowledge of ancient sites and customs. The most significant of these researchers as far as biblical studies was concerned was Konstantin von Tischendorf (1815–74), a German scholar in the employ of the Russian tsar. Between 1844 and 1859 he made a series of exciting discoveries in St Catherine's Monastery near Mount Sinai. What came to be known as *Codex Sinaiticus* was forty-four leaves of a fourth-century book containing the New Testament and some other writings in Greek. Tischendorf bought and published the codex with a translation. It could immediately be seen that it exposed more clearly than ever the weaknesses of the *Textus Receptus*, on which the Jacobean scholars had relied.

Codex Sinaiticus was the most important of the text discoveries which had been made since the seventeenth century, which would go on being made into the twentieth century, and which fuelled the argument for a major revision of the Authorized Version. Noah Webster, a son of the American Revolution, who had served the American language with his *American Dictionary of the English Language* (1806), later turned his attention to the Bible with his *Holy Bible, containing the Old and New Testaments, in the Common Version with Amendments of the Language* (1833). His object was to replace archaisms such as "sufficient unto the day is the evil thereof" (Matthew 6:34) with "words expressing the sense which is most common in popular usage". From about this time vigorous attempts were made by leading scholars to gain official sanction for a new version. In 1856 a group of leading churchmen appealed in vain for a royal commission to explore the possibility but it would be another fourteen years before any positive steps were taken. The Authorized Version had become such an icon that for many the prospect of altering it was little short of sacrilegious. The vigorous evangelical Christianity which held sway in nineteenth-century Britain was, in many ways, backward-looking. Just as the majority of newly built churches and chapels were in the Victorian Gothic style, with spires and arched windows, so most church people felt more comfortable with a Bible that spoke to them of long historical tradition. It was 1870 before a positive move was made to update the King James Version.

In that year Samuel Wilberforce, the bishop of Winchester, proposed to the southern Convocation of the Church of England that a committee be set up to report on the desirability of revising the Authorized Version. The suggestion was favourably received. The outcome was similar to that of 1603. Two teams were established, one to work on the Old Testament and one on the

New. The scholars then settled down to a task which would take them fifteen years to complete (the Apocrypha revision was not completed until 1896). What was different was that a group of American scholars were invited to be involved. Two parallel teams were set up in the USA. The terms of reference were cautious in the extreme and were headed by the injunction "To introduce as few alterations as possible into the Text of the Authorized Version consistently with faithfulness".

Hampered by such restrictions, the resulting text was never going to be very exciting. It was, especially in the New Testament, a word-for-word rendering of the original language. So eager were the translators to preserve the feel of the King James Version that, not only did they retain "thee" and "thou", they actually added in archaic words. "Peradventure", "aforetime", "haply", "us-ward", "howbeit" were just some of the already obsolete words the revisers sprinkled throughout their text. In several cases changes intended to clarify did just the reverse. Thus Jesus' exhortation "if thy right hand offend thee cut it off" (Matthew 5:30) needed to be amended because the word "offend" had changed its meaning over time. But to replace it with the vaguely ridiculous "if thy right hand causeth thee to stumble" was scarcely helpful. The Revised Version was certainly more accurate but it lacked the rhythm of the original. What the revisers ended up creating was the literary equivalent of a pseudo-Gothic cathedral.

It would be churlish to insist, however, that the Revised Version was totally without merit. One of its strong points was its rendering of Hebrew poetry. Although the old Bible had made a pretty good job of conveying Old Testament lyricism into English, there were passages in the King James Version which verged on the incomprehensible. Consider, for example, its rendering of Job 28:1–3:

(v.1) Surely there is a vein for the silver, and
a place for gold where they fine it.

(v.2) Iron is taken out of the earth, and

brass is molten out of the stone.

(v.3) He setteth an end to darkness, and searcheth out all
perfection: the stones of darkness, and the shadow of death.

The Revised Version set the passage out as poetry, which was
certainly a help. And it did make it clear that the writer was
describing mining activity:

(v.1) Surely there is a mine for silver,
And a place for gold which they refine.

(v.2) Iron is taken out of the earth,
And brass is molten out of the stone.

(v.3) Man setteth an end to darkness,
And searcheth out to the furthest bound
The stones of thick darkness and of the shadow of death.[1]

Unsurprisingly, the Americans were distinctly underwhelmed by
the work of their British partners. The drafts of the Revised Version
which they were shown were too stuffy. They presented their own
work to the British committee with a list of those amendments
they considered to be really essential. Unfortunately, compromise
proved impossible. The hand of the King James Version lay so
heavily on the project that Britain's best biblical scholars could not
allow themselves to think creatively. Translation inevitably involves
interpretation but the revisers lacked the freedom to convey
as vividly as possible the meaning of the originals. In the event
the Americans went their own way and published the American
Standard Version in 1901.

Conservatives pounced with glee on the shortcomings of the
new version. The most savage of the critics was John Burgon, dean
of Chichester. He was an archaeologist and biblical scholar of merit
but in the contempt he publicly poured on the Revised Version and
its compilers he allowed prejudice to run away with him:

*How it happened that, with so many splendid scholars
sitting round their table, they should have produced a
Translation which, for the most part, reads like a first-rate
school-boy's crib – tasteless, unlovely, harsh, unidiomatic;
servile without being really faithful – pedantic without
being really learned – an unreadable Translation, in
short; the result of a vast amount of labour indeed, but of
wondrous little skill – how all this has come about it were
utterly useless at this time of day to enquire.*[2]

What angered Burgon and those who thought like him was not
that the revisers had done a poor job but that they had done any
job at all.

We can have quite a lot of sympathy for the enemies of the Revised
Version because they, and all conservatively inclined Christians,
were living through stormy times which disposed them to cling to
the rock of the Authorized Version when they were buffeted by the
waves and winds of doubt and criticism. As Burgon complained,
"The effect which these ever-recurring announcements produce on
the devout reader of Scripture is the reverse of edifying; is never
helpful; is always bewildering."[3] The mid-century archbishop of
Dublin, Richard Whateley, spoke no less than the truth when he
told his diocesan conference that the King James Version was *not*
the Bible but a mere translation. Nevertheless his words profoundly
shocked the hearers.

One problem arose from those very advances in scholarship
which had made it possible to revise the biblical text. Discoveries of
early documents continued to be made. And a major breakthrough
was the Vatican's release of a photographic facsimile of *Codex
Vaticanus* in 1889–90. An extensive library of chronicles, law,
wisdom writings, prophetic literature, biography, letters, and poetry
compiled over more than a thousand years and under a wide range
of circumstances was now available for closer examination. By the
late nineteenth century scholars had accumulated the evidence and
developed the research skills to subject these texts to close scrutiny,
compare them with other ancient writings, and relate them to the

history and archaeology of the ancient world. Experts insisted that the sacred texts should be subjected to the same kind of scrutiny that would be directed at any classical and pre-classical documents. This approach had been known for a century as "higher criticism" to distinguish it from the "lower criticism" which was concerned solely with comparing variant texts in order to arrive at what was considered to be the earliest – and, therefore, the most reliable – reading. The centre of this radical theology was the University of Tübingen and the growing influence of the "Tübingen School" had, by the mid-nineteenth century, raised issues of great seriousness for the understanding and interpretation of the Bible. Its most devastating impact was on the Gospels. The radical German scholars and those who followed them insisted that the New Testament writers and the early church had built an elaborate theological structure on the foundation of the life and teaching of a great Jewish rabbi. In their attempts to distinguish "the Jesus of history" from "the Christ of faith" they tended to play down the miraculous and cast doubt on the Resurrection.

Liberals and Conservatives

The effect on the church was traumatic. The new school of biblical scholarship raised again, as the Reformation had done, in a different way, the issue of authority. Where was sinful, confused man wandering through this vale of tears to turn for certainty about things eternal? Believers in the Protestant world had confidently pinned their hopes on the infallible word of God written. Now its accuracy and, it seemed, its fundamental truths were being challenged. Thinking people, of course, responded in a variety of ways but in the English-speaking world they tended to fall into three broad categories.

Those who attempted to come to terms with the radical theology eventually attracted the name of "Liberals". They were concerned that not to do so would make the church appear obscurantist and irrelevant. "Hitherto," wrote Benjamin Jowett,

Oxford professor and Master of Balliol, "religion seems to have become more and more powerless among the educated classes. Do we not want a Gospel for the educated... not because it is more blessed to preach to the educated than to the poor, but because the faith of the educated is permanent and ultimately affects the faith of the poor?"[4] Leading Liberals were not abandoning the Bible; they believed that it contained divine truth but mediated through fallible human beings whose intellectual limitations tended to distort the message. How, then, was truth to be detected? By applying individual mental powers every student would arrive at what was truth for him/herself.

To many this seemed like a scandalous rejection of everything the church stood for. In 1860 Jowett was one member of a group of Liberals who published their ideas in a book entitled *Essays and Reviews*. The Anglican establishment was enraged. The only members of the group they could take action against were two beneficed clergy. They were examined for heresy and sacked (though restored on appeal). They were not the only ones to suffer as a result of the acrimonious biblical conflicts of the mid-Victorian years.

While the Liberals vested final authority in individual judgment, the Tractarians elevated the priesthood to that position. They reached back beyond the Reformation to a time when the Bible was not freely available to all and the clergy were both guardians of doctrine and intermediaries between the laity and God. This group of high churchmen derived their name from the *Tracts for the Times*, a series of pamphlets setting out their beliefs on a variety of doctrinal and liturgical issues. They believed that many of the problems facing the church had come about by making word more important than sacrament and encouraging untrained laymen to interpret the Bible for themselves. Although they valued the Scriptures, they were less vulnerable to the Liberal challenge because they did not regard the Bible as self-authenticating. For them the church (i.e. the ecclesiastical establishment) was the interpreter of Scripture and the definer of doctrine. No less than the Liberals, the Tractarians and those who shared their theological outlook aroused considerable hostility. Their sacerdotalism and their love of ritual suggested to their critics that they were no more than covert Roman Catholics (a suspicion confirmed when several leading Tractarians seceded to Rome).

The third group was made up of those church people, mainly but not exclusively evangelicals, who rejected all criticism of the Bible and continued to regard it as the unshakeable rock of their faith. Burgon was to the fore among this majority, declaring in *Inspiration and Interpretation* (1861),

> *The Bible is none other than the voice of Him that sitteth*
> *upon the throne. Every book of it, every chapter of it,*
> *every word of it, every syllable of it, every letter of it, is*
> *the direct utterance of the Most High. The Bible is none*
> *other than the Word of God, not some part of it more,*
> *some part of it less, but all alike the utterance of Him*
> *who sitteth upon the throne, faultless, unerring, supreme.*[5]

Three years later a conference of 150 clergy and academics issued the celebrated Oxford Declaration:

> *We, the undersigned presbyters and deacons in holy orders*
> *of the Church of England and Ireland hold it to be our*
> *bounden duty to the Church and to the souls of men, to*
> *declare our firm belief that the Church of England and*
> *Ireland, in common with the whole Catholic Church,*
> *maintains without reserve or qualification, the Inspiration*
> *and Divine Authority of the whole Canonical Scriptures,*
> *as not only containing but being, the Word of God; and*
> *further teaches in the words of our Blessed Lord, that the*
> *"punishment" of the "cursed" equally with the "life" of*
> *the "righteous" is "everlasting".*

The authors called on all British clergy to subscribe to this declaration and 11,000 did so. There was, however, a considerable party of dissent which believed that to tie all ministers of religion to such an uncompromising statement about biblical inerrancy and to deny the possibility of scholarly debate was dangerously obscurantist.

All this was happening at the same time – and overlapping with – the far better known evolution debate. Charles Darwin's *Origin of Species* appeared in 1859 and was followed twelve years later by his *Descent of Man*. The controversy unleashed by Darwin's revolutionary writings is too well known to require recitation here. It divided the nation from top to bottom, with William Ewart Gladstone (currently Chancellor of the Exchequer) declaring, "Upon the grounds of what is called evolution God is relieved of the labour of creation, and in the name of unchangeable laws is discharged from governing the world."

In June 1860 a debate took place in Oxford which has, ever since, been seen (rightly or wrongly) as one of the major events in the "religion versus science" conflict. Bishop Samuel Wilberforce did battle with Thomas Huxley over Darwin's theory of human evolution. It was one of the great confrontations of the age. More than a thousand turned up to hear it and many were turned away. Although both sides claimed victory, the consensus of opinion has always been that the scientist won. It is, however, interesting to record that Huxley always claimed that he was not anti-Bible. On the contrary, he regarded it as an indispensable part of the nation's culture. What he called for was a new edition purged of "error". He did not advocate, he said, "burning the ship to get rid of the cockroaches". It was a view which found some support among the Bible's most dedicated advocates. Charles Ellicott, bishop of Gloucester, who headed the revision committee working on the Revised New Testament, acted on the assumption that the best way to stifle criticism of the text was to acknowledge that transcription errors had crept in over the centuries and that once a "pure" translation had been achieved the church would be able to unite behind it.

However the background against which the scholars of the Revised Version had to do the work was one in which many Christians were extremely nervous about any tinkering with the age-old text. Preachers who did not hesitate to lump together as devil's spawn Darwin, Huxley, the Tübingen radicals, and all liberal theologians were scarcely less scathing of modernizers who wanted to lay their hands on the Authorized Version for educational and missionary purposes. The traditionalists were the spiritual heirs of those defenders of the Vulgate who had considered it their pious duty to dig up Wycliffe's bones and burn Tyndale. The nineteenth century came to an end with most British and American churches still using the King James Version and few setting much store by the result of the latest attempt to update it. Neither theologians nor scientists had dislodged it from its position in church, chapel, or home. Its position seemed secure as humanity stood on the doorstep of the most violent century in its history.

The Bible in a Changing World

In Britain the old social order was all but destroyed by World War I and its aftermath. No longer were many rural communities led by the squire and the vicar or urban centres dominated by the local factory owner. The appalling loss of life on the Western Front, where young soldiers were urged towards the barbed wire and the machine-gun posts by flag-waving padres who stayed safely behind the lines, did little to advance the Christian cause. Universal adult suffrage (1928), the spread of socialism, and the emergence of a Labour party capable of governing hacked away at the class system, which had been one of the buttresses of church attendance. What few old certainties remained were further undermined by the economic depression of the 1930s and World War II. When, in 1945, the electorate rejected the war hero, Winston Churchill, in favour of a Labour government, it was clear that more radical change was on the way. In subsequent decades, growing prosperity, more evenly shared, fuelled the secularization of society.

The social, intellectual, religious crisis of the 1960s was
specific to no one particular religious tradition... it was
not even a specifically religious crisis, it was rather one
of the total culture, affecting many secular institutions
in a way comparable to its effect on the churches. It was
a crisis of the relevance (or capacity for sheer survival)
of long-standing patterns of thought and institutions of
all sorts in a time of intense, and rather self-conscious,
modernisation.[6]

In what came to be called the "developing world", needs, perceptions, and hopes were very different. It follows that among Christianized people in the colonies attitudes to the Bible were different. In the countries of Africa and Asia, struggling towards independence, political radicals regarded the King James Version as part of the white man's imperial tool kit. Yet, at the same time, millions of ordinary people who had been thoroughly Christianized clung to it with a tenacity far greater than that of their European brothers and sisters. Many shared the Jesus-like experience expressed by one Nigerian poet:

We stand like
confused children,
umbilically connected to two civilizations.[7]

Christians in Third World rural communities identified far more easily with the biblical narrative than sophisticated Westerners. Famine, flood, epidemic, tribal warfare, infant mortality, and the simplicity of agrarian life were experiences with which they were as familiar as those who heard Amos preach or brought their sick children to Jesus. Their culture was based on recited stories, traditional praise songs, and tribal chronicles. They did not need to set Bible stories in historical or cultural contexts. They were *their* stories, through which God spoke directly. Many people read the Bible in their own language but the fortunate few who had a good education (and were, therefore, destined to be the leaders of newly independent nations) spoke the lingua franca of the colonizers. As a result the King James Bible was read, studied, learned, and loved in all corners of the British empire. Independence did not change people's devotion towards it. They did not question its accuracy; indeed to do so was regarded as blasphemous; nor did they recognize any need for its language to be updated. If they were (and still are) biblical fundamentalists, it was because they identified intimately with the text – something not always appreciated by Western critics.

It was the Western world that was turning its back on Christianity. Church attendances steadily declined and new laws restricted the propagation of religion in schools. When legislators ordained that the Bible was not to be taught in class or used in assemblies as *the* truth, they were knocking away one of the major props supporting traditional society. For the first time in over three centuries, generations of British people reached adulthood without experiencing much exposure to the Authorized Version of the Bible. For the majority of Elizabeth II's subjects who thought about it at all, this book was old-fashioned and associated with a religion which was largely irrelevant.

The churches were fully aware of the challenge and made determined efforts to modernize. They adopted new liturgies – not without considerable internal conflict. Even the Roman Catholic Church abandoned its exclusive commitment to the Latin mass. For a couple of decades "ecumenism" was the buzz word as once-rival communions grew closer together to confront the common enemy of secularism. Worship in the modern vernacular and the quest for new tools to equip the late twentieth-century church for its mission created a demand for a Bible in modern English. But which one?

Pre-World War II Translations

One of the intriguing features of the story of the Bible is the large number of vernacular versions that have been written. In English alone there has been a continuous stream of new translations from the mid-seventeenth century onwards. It is not our task to describe any of them except insofar as they relate to the story of the King James Version. Ferrar Fenton's *Holy Bible in Modern English containing the complete sacred scriptures of the Old and New Testaments translated into English direct from the original Hebrew, Chaldaic and Greek* qualifies by virtue of its dedicatory epistle. Fenton was a wealthy businessman and self-taught biblical scholar. His eccentric version, which for a time proved very popular, was completed in 1903 and dedicated, he said, to

> *All those nations who have sprung from the race of the British Isles, and to whom the English language, in its developed power, is the mother tongue; and with them to all the inhabitants of the world to whom English has become, or may become, the language of thought, in hope that a clear presentment of the laws of creation and human existence will restore them from the mental distress of atheistic doubt, to a firm reliance upon God, their Creator, and the practice of His revealed laws of life, bodily and spiritual.*[8]

Fenton set himself single-handedly to challenge the Darwinians and the higher critics and also to produce a new masterpiece in the English language which would replace the long-esteemed King James Version. For many readers it seems to have succeeded in its objective, for it continued in print until 1944.

James Moffatt set himself to do just the opposite. He refused to be influenced by the language and cadences of the seventeenth-century Bible and to maximize the impact of his translation by using language which was, by the standards of the day, quite racy. This prominent Scottish academic, who ended his career as professor of church history at Union Theological Seminary, New York, published the New Testament in 1913, the Old Testament in 1924, and the whole Bible in 1928. His gutsy language appealed to many because it seemed to convey the spirit of what the King

James Version was trying to say but not quite managing. For example, where the older version of the Song of Solomon 2:13 had "Arise, my love, my fair one, and come away", Moffatt wrote, "Come dear, come away, my beauty!" But he went further than just updating the language. He was not above tinkering with the text in order to make it, in his view, more intelligible, without the backing of any early evidence. Thus he moved chapters 15–16 of John's Gospel so that they followed on from John 13:21. This provided a more logical order for Jesus' address at the Last Supper. It is the kind of change a lecturer (such as Moffatt) might make in going over his notes before delivering an address but it does not happen to agree with any ancient source. It must have been his Scottish Free Church sensibilities that drove him to relegate to a footnote Paul's advice to his young protégé in 1 Timothy 5:23: "Take a little wine for the sake of your stomach and your frequent attacks of illness."

Post-World War II Translations

In the USA it took little more than a generation for the powers that be to decide that the American Standard Version of 1901 needed updating. The copyright holders, the International Council of Religious Education, recommended in 1930 that a committee be set up to thoroughly revise the revision. In 1937 thirty-two scholars set about the work. The Revised Standard Version of the New Testament appeared in 1946 and was followed by the Old Testament six years later. The committee tried hard to appeal to all constituencies in the church. In their preface they paid tribute to the King James Version, "the noblest monument of English prose", which had "entered, as no other book has, into the making of the personal character and the public institution of the English-speaking peoples". They decreed that the new work should "embody the best results of modern scholarship as to the meaning of the Scriptures, and express the meaning in English diction which is designed for use in public and private worship and preserve those qualities which have given to the King James Version a supreme place in English literature".

The Revised Standard Version was thus a Janus book, looking simultaneously in two directions. What the translators set themselves was an impossible task. To produce the best modern translation they would have had to slip the leash which bound them to the King James Version. To have been so bold would have been to court commercial disaster. For a time the new book was remarkably successful. It made a greater impact, on both sides of the Atlantic, than any of the other recent translations. This was partly due to timing. The Western church was looking for a new handbook for a new, post-war age. The Revised Standard Version with its outlawing of "thee" and "thou" seemed to fit the bill. Yet, at the same time, it did not tread on the toes of conservatives. The new Bible followed the rhythm of the old so closely that most readers would be scarcely aware of any difference. Compare, for example, the Sermon on the Mount (Matthew 5) in both versions:

KING JAMES VERSION

> *Blessed are the poor in spirit: for theirs is the kingdom of heaven.*
>
> *Blessed are they that mourn: for they shall be comforted.*
>
> *Blessed are the meek: for they shall inherit the earth.*
>
> *Blessed are they which do hunger and thirst after righteousness: for they shall be filled.*
>
> *Blessed are the merciful: for they shall obtain mercy.*
>
> *Blessed are the pure in heart: for they shall see God.*

REVISED STANDARD VERSION

> *"Blessed are the poor in spirit, for theirs is the kingdom of heaven.*

> *"Blessed are those who mourn, for they shall be comforted.*

> *"Blessed are the meek, for they shall inherit the earth.*

> *"Blessed are those who hunger and thirst for righteousness, for they shall be satisfied.*

> *"Blessed are the merciful, for they shall obtain mercy.*

> *"Blessed are the pure in heart, for they shall see God."*

The new Bible even retained a glaring archaism a few lines further on when it read "Nor do men light a lamp and put it under a bushel."

The publishers of the new translations even tried to win support by giving it the physical appearance of the King James Version. People looking for a "real" Bible, perhaps to give as a confirmation or baptism present, wanted a book in a smart slip case, on India paper with the text set out in two columns and a centre panel for cross references. This is what the publishers of the Revised Standard Version gave them. To have diverged from the familiar would, as they knew, have had a disastrous effect on sales.

In the first ten years of its existence the Revised Standard Version sold more than 12 million copies. Had the last word in English vernacular Scripture been uttered? Anyone who has followed the troubled story of the King James Version thus far will guess the answer to that question. A Bible that tried to be all things to all men was bound to end up offending some. Inevitably, there were those who thought it too tame and others who found it too bold. One reactionary American preacher stood in the pulpit and dramatically took a blow torch to a copy of the new book.

The world was moving too fast for the Revised Standard Version to hold the ring permanently. Other translations continued to appear. By the late 1970s students enjoyed an *embarras de richesses*. Probably the most useful texts were those designed for a restricted clientele whose compilers were not looking over their shoulders at the events of 1603–11. The Second Vatican Council of the Roman Catholic Church (1962–65) promoted wide-ranging reforms, including the increased use of vernacular worship. This, in turn, implied increased use of vernacular Scriptures. Moves had been afoot ever since the Second World War to provide new Bibles for the Catholic world. The best, the Jerusalem Bible, appeared first in French (1954) and in English in 1966. Of course, nowhere in its ancestry does the King James Version appear. Yet it is, perhaps, the Jerusalem Bible that comes closest to it in terms of musicality and suitability for reading in worship. Compare, for example, the colourful and dramatic openings of Isaiah 6.

King James Version

*(v. 1) In the year that king Uzziah died I saw
also the Lord sitting upon a throne, high and
lifted up, and his train filled the temple.*

*(v. 2) Above it stood the seraphims: each one had six
wings; with twain he covered his face, and with twain
he covered his feet, and with twain he did fly.*

*(v. 3) And one cried unto another, and said, Holy, holy, holy,
is the Lord of hosts: the whole earth is full of his glory.*

Jerusalem Bible

*(v. 1) In the year of King Uzziah's death I saw the Lord
Yahweh seated on a high throne; his train filled the sanctuary;
(v. 2) above him stood seraphs, each one with six wings: two
to cover its face, two to cover its feet and two for flying.*

(v.3) And they cried out one to another in this way,
"Holy, holy, holy is Yahweh Sabaoth.
His glory fills the whole earth."

Another post-war treatment of the sacred text deliberately turned its back on the 1611 version. J. B. Phillips (see p. 111), a London vicar, resolved "to 'forget' completely the majesty and beauty of the Authorised Version" and "translate the Greek text as one would translate any other document from a foreign language, with the same conscientiousness but also with the same freedom in conveying, as far as possible, the meaning and style of the original writer".[9] Phillips set out to paraphrase the New Testament, beginning with the epistles (*Letters to Young Churches*, 1947) and completing the project in 1958. At first these paraphrases seemed excitingly daring and were immediately popular. Within a couple of years *Letters to Young Churches* sold 4.25 million copies. It is not difficult to see why. Students wrestling with the compact thought of the apostle Paul might seriously scratch their heads over such passages as Romans 4:1–5 in the King James Version:

(v.1) What shall we say then that Abraham our
father, as pertaining to the flesh, hath found?

(v.2) For if Abraham were justified by works, he
hath whereof to glory, but not before God.

(v.3) For what saith the scripture? Abraham believed
God, and it was counted unto him for righteousness.

(v.4) Now to him that worketh is the reward
not reckoned of grace, but of debt.

(v.5) But to him that worketh not, but believeth on him that
justifieth the ungodly, his faith is counted for righteousness.

It is with a sigh of relief that readers might turn to Phillips's treatment:

> *(v.1) Now how does all this affect the position of our ancestor Abraham? (v.2) Well, if justification were by achievement he could quite fairly be proud of what he achieved – but not, I am sure, proud before God. (v.3) For what does the Scripture say about him? And Abraham believed God, and it was reckoned unto him for righteousness.*

> *(v.4) Now if a man works his wages are not counted as a gift but as a fair reward. (v.5) But if a man, irrespective of his work, has faith in Him who justifies the sinful, then that man's faith is counted as righteousness, and that is the gift of God. This is the happy state of the man whom God accounts righteous, apart from his achievements.*

In the 1960s two major translations were being worked on simultaneously. In Britain teams of scholars under the aegis of the university presses of Cambridge and Oxford worked on what was to be a "thoroughly modern" English Bible. In their determination not to be in thrall to the King James Version the translators of the New English Bible used idiomatic language that was at times racy. They published in 1970. Six years later the Good News Bible came from the USA (though the English and Scottish Bible societies were represented on the committee). Less radical in its modernisms, this offered the reader a text broken up with subheadings and illustrated with line engravings.

Every new translation to come off the press had its supporters but all had their detractors – people for whom the King James Version was, and would always remain, the last word. One critic, writing in a Canadian newspaper, grumbled,

> *The translations go wrong because of a mistaken belief that the Bible "must be presented in language that is direct and plain and meaningful to people today" in the words of*

the introduction to… the New Revised Standard Version.

It has not satisfied those who would like a truly vibrant contemporary English translation, and numerous other attempts have been made. Typical of these attempts is the New English Bible, completed in 1970, a truly wretched attempt to render the language of the Bible into "contemporary English". It has some of the most flat, uninspired phrasing ever produced by translators with ears of tin. The Jerusalem Bible, read in Canadian Catholic churches, is just as awful.[10]

The most successful translation in the Protestant world to date has proved to be the New International Version (lampooned by some as the "Nearly Inspired Version"). This evangelical enterprise had its beginnings in the USA in 1965 but an international and interdenominational team were involved in the translation. What most closely connects the New International Version with the King James Version is the way the translators went about their task. They were "united in their commitment to the authority and infallibility of the Bible as God's Word in written form". In that they were at one with their Jacobean scholarly ancestors. Their methodology was also very similar.

The translation of each book was assigned to a team of scholars. Next, one of the Intermediate Editorial Committees revised the initial translation, with constant reference to the Hebrew, Aramaic, or Greek. Their work then went to one of the General Editorial Committees, which checked it in detail and made another thorough revision. This revision in turn was carefully reviewed by the Committee on Bible Translation, which made further changes and then released the final version for publication. In this way the entire Bible underwent three revisions, during each of which the translation was examined for its faithfulness to the original languages and for its English style.

All this involved many thousands of hours of research and discussion regarding the meaning of the texts and the precise way of putting them into English.

A sensitive feeling for style does not always accompany scholarship. Accordingly the Committee on Bible Translation submitted the developing version to a number of stylistic consultants. Two of them read every book of both Old and New Testaments twice – once before and once after the last major revision – and made invaluable suggestions. Samples of the translations were tested for clarity and ease of reading by various kinds of people – young and old, highly educated and less well educated, ministers and laymen.

The committee were proud of their work, which was finally completed in 1978 and concluded:

> *It may well be that no other translation has been made*
> *by a more thorough process of review and revision from*
> *committee to committee than this one.*[11]

Archbishop Bancroft and his colleagues might have had something to say about that.

CHAPTER 10

INSPIRATION AND
IDOLATRY

Four centuries have come and gone since James I's team of translators completed their mammoth task. How might they respond to the discovery that their book was still being bought and sold in its millions, that there were churches where it continued to feature in Sunday-by-Sunday worship, that there were some church people who refused to countenance any other version, and that there were literary gurus – many of whom would not own up to being Christians – who placed the King James Version on a pedestal and criticized the Church for abandoning it? Would they be flattered, gratified? They would certainly be pleased to know that their version had been a conduit carrying the word of God to the four corners of the world. But some, perhaps all, would, I feel sure, be appalled by other aspects of the King James Version story. They might protest, "We did not labour all those months merely to create a revered literary masterpiece. We strove, albeit inadequately, to offer to God and his worshippers in our own time the best version of Holy Scripture in English that we could devise."

Scholars and intellectuals as they were, they would have acknowledged that society changes and that the church must change also – not with the world but for the world. I doubt whether Bancroft's men realized that they stood at such a watershed in the history of the English-speaking peoples; that England was emerging as the leading Protestant nation; and that thousands of their fellow countrymen, armed with the Authorized Version, would leave their homeland to propagate their culture and their religion so widely and so dramatically.

We, of course, do know these things. All we have to do is interpret them! The questions we must ask ourselves are: what was – and is – the King James Version for and how well has it fulfilled – and is it fulfilling – its task?

The new translation was meant to be a focus of unity. It would achieve this by being set firmly in a liturgical context where its interpretation and application were securely in the hands of the bishops and their appointees. Did it succeed in this? Well, yes and no. The King James Version became, for over three centuries, *the* Bible of the English-speaking world. But those united in using it were not united in interpreting or applying it. Historian Jacques Barzun astutely observed, "The 16th C literature of Bible argument and foul invective began what we now call the popularization of ideas through the first of the mass media."[1] That process could not be stopped by driving rival Scripture texts from the market.

The more people thought for themselves throughout the ensuing decades, the more likely they were to challenge old authorities, old customs, old religious doctrines, old beliefs. Clerics of all parties complained that lay people no longer accorded them the respect to which they believed their standing and their education entitled them. Anyone armed with a Bible might challenge what he or she heard in the pulpit. And there were many laymen who understood the word of God better than their clergy and ministers. In 1643 the elderly jurist and MP, John Selden, attended a conference of divines at Westminster and frequently interrupted the proceedings to correct the churchmen on points of fact or interpretation. "Perhaps in your little pocket-Bibles with gilt leaves the translation may be thus," he insisted, "but the Greek or the Hebrew signifies thus and thus."[2]

Those in power in church and state could not allow incipient revolution to go unchallenged. The Christian commonwealth had to be indivisible. There could be no question of allowing groups of dissidents to believe and worship as they wished. Crown and mitre stood or fell together, as James I knew very well and expressed very forcefully. But many people would not be dragooned into uniformity. Thousands migrated to set up their own churches in foreign lands and, within England, several Nonconformist assemblies had diverged from the state church within a century, despite persecution. On major issues Christians who disagreed with each other used the same Bible to bolster their arguments. Parliamentarian and royalist preachers threw proof texts at each other. So did the defenders and opponents of slavery during the American Civil War.

What Bancroft's men did not realize or refused to accept was that the Bible was a manual for revolution. Wycliffe and Erasmus and Luther had all been right. They had prophesied that once the word of God was made available for all to read, it would change the church and change society with scant need for human intervention. The open word of God was like a powerful mastiff on a leash held by the ecclesiastical authorities. In 1604 those interested in revising the vernacular Bible fell, broadly speaking, into two camps. There were those who wanted to make it yet more effective. They sought, as it were, to lengthen the leash. Others were more concerned to bring the hound under tighter control, to ensure that it was thoroughly domesticated and made *safe*. This could be achieved by removing all contentious glosses. It could be achieved by encasing the word within the liturgy.

The King James Version as Literature

In later centuries those who also wanted to tame the word of God locked it in a cage called "literature". Now, it is possible to take the King James Bible out of its historical and religious context and assess its value as an enduring cultural artefact. It makes little sense to do so and any judgment we might make as to the book's literary merit will be largely subjective. But let us play the game for the moment and consider what criteria we might use.

First of all, how does the 1611 Bible stand up to comparison with other contemporary English masterpieces? The Renaissance of letters was in spate when King James came to the throne. The literary giants of the age, such as Shakespeare, Ben Jonson, John Donne, and Francis Bacon, were well known by reputation and, in some instances personally, to the translators. Some of the academics lived in London and were habitués of the royal court, and even those who resided in Oxford and Cambridge travelled occasionally to the capital. They could not avoid being influenced by the cultural climate. If we take a few contemporary examples almost at random, we shall see two things – how linguistically similar they are to the 1611 Bible and also how the Bible shaped the thought patterns of their authors. Here is a passage from Francis Bacon's essay *On Adversity*:

> *Prosperity is the blessing of the Old Testament, adversity is the blessing of the New, which carrieth the greater benediction, and the clearer revelation of God's favour. Yet even in the Old Testament, if you listen to David's harp, you shall hear as many hearse-like airs as carols; and the pencil of the Holy Ghost hath laboured more in describing the afflictions of Job than the felicities of Solomon.*

A sermon by John Donne directed to the fashionable atheist has all the ringing, spellbinding oratory of an Old Testament prophet:

Bee as confident as thou canst, in company; for company
is the Atheists Sanctuary; I respit thee not till the day of
Judgement, when I may see thee upon thy knees, upon
thy face, begging of the hills, that they would fall downe
and cover thee from the fierce wrath of God, to aske thee
then, Is there a God now? I respit thee not till the day of
thine own death, when thou shalt have evidence enough,
that there is a God, though no other evidence, but to finde
a Devill, and evidence enough, that there is a Heaven,
though no other evidence, but to feele Hell; to aske thee
then, Is there a God now? I respit thee but a few houres,
but six houres, but till midnight. Wake then; and then
darke, and alone, Heare God aske thee then, remember
that I asked thee now, Is there a God? And if thou darest,
say No.[3]

Or consider the gentleman poet Francis Quarles (1592–1644). Though little known now, he was immensely popular and influential in his own day.

And what's a life? A weary pilgrimage,
Whose glory in one day doth fill thy stage
With childhood, manhood, and decrepit age.

And what's a life? The flourishing array
Of the proud summer-meadow, which to-day
Wears her green plush, and is to-morrow hay.[4]

The allusion is to Luke 12:28, "If then God so clothe the grass, which is to day in the field and to morrow is cast into the oven; how much more will he clothe you...?"

In Jacobean England the rival to the pulpit was the stage. Ben Jonson knew that effectiveness in either arena was dependent on addressing the human condition in language at once simple and vibrant. He rejected the high bombast of Elizabethan tragedy and the mock battles fought out within the Globe Theatre's "wooden O".

He rather prays you will be pleas'd to see
One such to-day, as other plays should be;
Where neither chorus wafts you o'er the seas,
Nor creaking throne comes down the boys to please;
Nor nimble squib is seen to make afeard
The gentlewoman; nor roll'd bullet heard
To say, it thunders; nor tempestuous drum
Rumbles, to tell you when the storm doth come;
But deeds, and language, such as men do use...[5]

Nor was it only the literary giants of the age who shared in the flowering of late Renaissance letters. Polemical pamphlets, diplomatic correspondence, and much written communication between educated men reveals a love of words and exuberant and inventive use made of them.

Bancroft's men and contemporary poets and dramatists breathed the same literary air and one chemical component of it was the Bible. It would, therefore, be surprising if there were no stylistic comparisons between the sacred text and works written for the cultural elite and the play-going public. The description of the new Jerusalem in Revelation 21: 4 would not be out of place as a Shakespearian monologue:

And I saw a new heaven and a new earth: for the first
heaven and the first earth were passed away; and there
was no more sea. And I John saw the holy city, new
Jerusalem, coming down from God out of heaven,
prepared as a bride adorned for her husband. And I heard
a great voice out of heaven saying, Behold, the tabernacle
of God is with men, and he will dwell with them, and
they shall be his people, and God himself shall be with
them, and be their God. And God shall wipe away all
tears from their eyes; and there shall be no more death,
neither sorrow, nor crying, neither shall there be any more
pain; for the former things are passed away.

Stylistically, then, the King James Version is of its age and bears comparison with the best of contemporary writings. But, while style is transient, substance (especially biblical substance) is perdurable. Alexander Pope published his *Essay on Criticism* exactly one hundred years after the appearance of the 1611 Bible. In it he satirized the fashionable tendency to value presentation more highly than content:

> *Others for Language all their Care express,*
> *And value Books, as Women Men, for Dress:*
> *Their Praise is still – The Stile is excellent:*
> *The Sense, they humbly take upon Content.*
> *Words are like Leaves; and where they most abound,*
> *Much Fruit of Sense beneath is rarely found.*

He castigated the empty-headedness of people who read poetry,

> *... but to please their Ear,*
> *Not mend their Minds, as some to Church repair,*
> *Not for the Doctrine, but the Musick there.*

Times change and if it is difficult to see clearly the focus of Pope's criticism, it may be because, in twenty-first-century Britain, there are few people who attend church on anything like a regular basis for aesthetic satisfaction and expect the Scripture readings to be taken from the King James Version. Even in most English cathedrals and great collegiate chapels the 1611 Bible has been dethroned in favour of more modern texts. However, for a wide variety of reasons, throughout the eighteenth and nineteenth centuries the King James Version enjoyed a special place in the affections of English-speaking peoples and certainly saw off all attempts to replace it with new translations and paraphrases. As decades lengthened into centuries, whatever faults were apparent to various scholars, the Bible which had served generations of Christians held the affections of the vast majority. To Lord Macaulay, writing in 1828, it was "that stupendous work", and, as we have seen, he applauded its economy of style and its extensive vocabulary (see p. 153). The King James Version had assumed the character of a wise and dignified elderly uncle whose eccentricities were tolerated out of affection and respect. Familiarity was important. Whether the worshipper attended church or chapel, he knew that Sunday by Sunday, the same book would be opened, the book he had grown up with, the book whose stories had become increasingly familiar to him as the years passed. Children learned verses by heart in school and Sunday school and many continued the habit into adulthood.

Religious Change in the Nineteenth Century

It is an idyllic picture and, like all idylls, it is only partially true. Archibald Campbell Tait, archbishop of Canterbury (1811–82), described the Church of England in 1876 as "an instrument devised by Providence for welding this great people into one compact Christian body".[6] The reality was far more complex. Throughout the nineteenth century more churches, chapels, and mission halls were built than in any previous comparable period. There were more clergy and ministers and they were better trained than ever before. There were periodic and very successful religious revivals. The Salvation Army was just the best known of evangelistic and social agencies working among the urban poor. Yet, despite all this vigorous activity, the proportion of the population which was unchurched grew, as did the gap between the privileged sections of society and the underclass of those (particularly in the industrial centres) who struggled to earn a subsistence wage and who lived in the jerry-built squalor of dark-roomed towns. An aristocratic friend of Selina, Countess of Huntingdon saw a wide chasm between herself and the underclass and resented preachers who presumed to question it. "It is monstrous," she exploded, "to be told you have a heart as sinful as the common wretches that crawl on the earth."[7] Most of the "common wretches" seldom went to church and certainly could not afford the luxury of owning a Bible.

An exception that neatly proves the rule was John Nicholas Tom

(1790–1838), a deluded rabble-rouser who went under a number of assumed names such as Count Moses Rothschild, Sir William Courtenay, the King of Jerusalem, and the true Messiah. This madman had an impressive bearing and was an effective orator. He also knew (or, at least, could quote – which is not necessarily the same thing) his Bible. When he addressed large crowds of the convinced and the curious, he knew what grievances to play on. His favourite text was James 5:1–8:

> *Go to now, ye rich men, weep and howl for your miseries that shall come upon you. Your riches are corrupted, and your garments are moth-eaten. Your gold and silver is cankered; and the rust of them shall be a witness against you, and shall eat your flesh as it were fire. Ye have heaped treasure together for the last days. Behold, the hire of the labourers who have reaped down your fields, which is of you kept back by fraud, crieth: and the cries of them which have reaped are entered into the ears of the Lord of Sabaoth. Ye have lived in pleasure on the earth, and been wanton; ye have nourished your hearts, as in a day of slaughter. Ye have condemned and killed the just; and he doth not resist you… Be ye also patient; stablish your hearts: for the coming of the Lord draweth nigh.*

In the newspaper he published, called *The Lion*, Tom castigated the religious establishment:

> *The Root of all Evil is in the Church*
>
> *Lucre! Lucre! Lucre!*
> *Heaven protect the Widow, Fatherless and Distressed.*

Tom's main centre of operation was Kent, where he had a large following. One farm labourer said of him, "He talked in such a manner to [his disciples] and was always reading the Scripture, that they did not look upon him as a common man and would have cheerfully died for his sake."[8] Some did, indeed, die for him and with him. The end of Tom's mad career came on a May afternoon in 1838. Two companies of soldiers were sent to arrest him and his followers. The "messiah" and a dozen of his disciples fell in a hail of bullets on a Kentish hillside. Tom's movement has been called the last peasants' revolt in English history.

Of course, the other side of the coin is that this same Bible over and again in the eighteenth and nineteenth centuries inspired Christians to tackle those very social ills against which Tom and other revolutionaries ranted. The work of Elizabeth Fry, Lord Shaftesbury, William Wilberforce, William Booth, and numerous others are well enough known to require no repetition. But such reformers were not representative of their class. For every churchgoer who felt his or her conscience stirred by what the Bible has to say about love, justice, and care for the poor there were hundreds who regarded the book as one of the major props of the *status quo*. They looked to it for confirmation of what they already believed. They looked to it for comfort in times of personal or national crisis. They were stirred by it to numerous acts of paternalistic charity. What they did not look to it for was any challenge which might have impelled them to change a society with which they were very comfortable. The magisterially confirming and comforting King James Version which had lain on their church or chapel lectern from time immemorial symbolized stability, social order, and, above all, changelessness.

The King James Version and the English Language

But, to return to a consideration of the Bible as literature, another touchstone we might apply in assessing the enduring worth of the King James Version is its lasting influence on the English language. A century ago a writer in the *Cambridge History of English Literature* cited as evidence of the Authorized Version's claim to be classified as a literary gem the large number of phrases from it that had passed into common parlance. It was an interesting list. One could not argue with "clear as crystal" or "sweat of his brow" or "the fat of the land". But familiarity, in itself, is not proof of quality. For two and a half centuries the Authorized Bible was the most widely read book. Many people, indeed, did not read any other. Whether they studied the Bible for themselves or not, they had it recited to them Sunday-by-Sunday in church. It would be surprising, indeed, if hundreds of biblical phrases had not become part of everyday conversation. What is interesting is the number of biblical phrases that have passed *out* of common usage over the last century. The list put forward in the 1909 edition of the *Cambridge History of English Literature*[9] included "highways and hedges", "the nether millstone", "dark sayings", "a word in season". Such terms have, with the passage of time and the secularization of society, become much less familiar. Once a phrase becomes lodged in the common psyche it does not have guaranteed longevity. To a large degree the survival of biblical expressions is dependent on the number of people still encountering them in the original text.

Similar considerations arise when we consult the *Oxford Dictionary of Quotations*. The fifth edition of that compendium offers us forty-one pages of King James Version aphorisms (as against fifty-one pages devoted to Shakespeare). We consult the dictionary when we want to check the exact wording of some half-remembered phrase or add weight to an observation of our own. We may well be grateful to discover "Saul and Jonathan were lovely and pleasant in their lives, and in their deaths they were not divided" (2 Samuel 1:23) or "Come unto me, all ye that labour and are heavy laden, and I will give you rest" (Matthew 11:28). But it would be difficult to find a use for "Jeshurun waxed fat and kicked" (Deuteronomy 32:15) or "superfluity of naughtiness" (James 1:21). One reason why so many Authorized Version phrases, once beloved of readers and hearers, have been consigned to the linguistic lumber room is to be found in the changes that have come over education techniques. Political correctness has removed the Bible from the centre to the fringes of school life. Learning by rote is now frowned on, so that children's minds no longer become treasure stores, filled with poems and

Bible verses. It must have been thirty or more years ago that I was speaking to the vice chancellor of an English university, who was bewailing the fact that the Authorized Version was no longer part of the intellectual equipment with which young students arrived. One result was that Milton's *Paradise Lost* could no longer be included in the first-year English course because undergraduates lacked the biblical foundation on which to base their study.

That leads us to the much more difficult question of how far the mellifluous cadences, simple syntax, and straightforward vocabulary of the King James Version can be discerned as influence on contemporary literary masters. It is, perhaps, significant that William Golding, the most Christian (or, at least, theological) of twentieth-century authors, chose as the theme of his first novel, *Lord of the Flies*, the story of a group of choirboys who, when marooned on a desert island, reverted to primeval savagery. Written within a decade of World War II, it breathed the disillusionment of an age which had shocked itself with its own propensity for evil. Other writers, particularly those who wrote for the stage, turned their backs angrily on old social conventions – and also on earlier literary conventions. Plays such as John Osborne's *Look Back in Anger* and Arnold Wesker's *Roots* were aggressively anti class structures and self-consciously anarchic. In one of Brendan Behan's plays an old lag reminisces about prison:

> *Many's the time the Bible was a consolation to a fellow alone in the old cell. The lovely thin paper with a bit of mattress coir in it, and if you could get a match… it was as good a smoke as ever I tasted.*[10]

In their development of style as well as subject matter, poets, novelists, and playwrights rejected very firmly the ordered, structured pre-1939 world. Bible-based morality had no place among the literary avant-garde and any linguistic elegance which might claim the Authorized Version among its ancestry was certainly to be shunned. Books, plays, poems had a jangling, jagged, inharmonious down-to-earthiness. Even lyric poets found their love of the musicality of words driven into harsh discordance by the need to repel old certainties – whether social or religious.

> *Do not go gentle into that good night, …*
> *Rage, rage against the dying of the light.*[11]

For more than half a century there has been little nostalgia for the King James Bible among those who shape the written language.

The Bible and Shakespeare

Those who put the Jacobean translation on a pedestal alongside the works of Shakespeare, in effect, concede that it does not readily speak to modern minds. Shakespeare is very much an acquired taste – *and so is the King James Version*. Shakespeare is difficult, as most school children exposed to him soon discover. *So is the King James Version*. To perpetuate the "Bible and Shakespeare" myth is to confuse what the two were about and it is rather tough on Shakespeare. The Bard of Avon was an individual genius with unique gifts of human understanding and poetic flair. The translators of the Bible were many and they did not between them produce a single original thought. That was not what they set out to do. On the contrary, they had to ensure that their own ideas did not interfere with the integrity of their translation. Shakespeare wrote to entertain, inspire, provoke reflection – and to make money. Bancroft's team were embarked on a pious mission to take sacred texts written at other times and in other cultures and make them relevant for their contemporaries as the divine revelation on which people ought to base their lives. Between the two there lies a wide gulf of both motivation and achievement. Shakespeare's plays and poems are sacrosanct. They are both of their time and timeless. Many would object to rendering *The Tempest* or *A Midsummer Night's Dream* into modern English to make it more acceptable to today's theatre-goers. Modern producers sometimes set the plays in a different time frame to help theatregoers appreciate their relevance but they would not dream of interfering with the text. The language, the thought forms, the literary conventions are those of an age long gone. The same might be said of Milton's *Samson Agonistes*, William Hobbes's *Leviathan* or William Blake's *Songs of Innocence*. Context is vital when we seek to understand great works of literature. By contrast, the Bible is a book that has, throughout its lifetime, been constantly translated so that, in public worship and private devotion, it might be "understanded of the people".[12] It was precisely for this purpose that Wycliffe, Tyndale, Coverdale, the Bancroft team, and other translators devoted so much time and energy to their chosen task. Beyond doubt, it helps a believer's understanding if he or she knows something of the time and circumstances in which various biblical books were written but he or she comes to the Bible not as a literary or historical artefact but as, to quote the British coronation service, the "lively Oracles of God". To claim that the very words of the King James Version should be treated with the same reverence as that accorded to Shakespeare's oeuvres is to be guilty of muddled thinking.

The Bible and Cultural Change

Today's culture has been shaped and is being shaped less by written works and much more by radio, film, television, and, of course, the internet. These media, almost by definition, use the language of everyday – of the street, the pub, and the office. For all these reasons, people's ears are far less used to hearing the seventeenth-century poetry and prose of the King James Version than was the case of all previous generations back to 1611. The words of the Authorized Bible become progressively less familiar with each succeeding year.

The churches are partly responsible for this, although it is difficult to see what they could have done to arrest the decline. Older Christians can remember the time when their infant faith was nurtured by the King James Bible or the Revised Standard Version translation, which was very close to it. Modern versions

are both numerous and less memorable. One internet site, www.
biblegateway.com, provides those who consult it with no fewer
than twenty alternative English translations. Most linguistic and
theological scholars, we may assume, offer their labours to the church
in a constructive spirit but it would be difficult for them to banish
entirely from their minds an attitude of competition. For example,
God's Word, produced under the auspices of the God's Word to the
Nations Bible Society (revised edition 1995), is promoted by the
slogan "The translation that says what it means". The implication,
presumably, is that other versions are less accurate.

In fact, the *God's Word* translation has been challenged on the
internet in ways worth quoting because they echo the concerns
expressed by the scholars of 1604 and, indeed, as far back as
Tyndale. The Reverend Jack Cascione, an American Lutheran
pastor, pointed out that

> *The first edition of "God's Word" retranslated all the
> passages in the New Testament that should say "by faith"
> or "through faith" into "because of faith", thus making
> our faith, instead of Christ, the cause of our salvation.
> Faith is not a human work or cause but it receives Christ's
> work.*
>
> *In this critic's opinion, the first edition of "God's Word"
> and the new revised edition continue to obscure the doctrine
> of justification by replacing the translation of all of the
> different Greek words behind "justify", "righteousness",
> "reckoned", "imputed", "accredited", and "propitiation"
> with one catch-all word, "approval".*
>
> *We understand the philosophy of making a translation
> easier to read. However, this has also led to a translation
> that is anything but a "study Bible". Couldn't they find six
> new words to consistently replace "justify", "righteousness",
> "reckoned", "imputed", "accredited", and "propitiation"?
> Must all be translated as "approval"?*
>
> *The first edition had blatantly taught false doctrine
> about "faith".* [13]

Subsequent editions of *God's Word* were duly corrected but it borders on the ironic that an evangelical publisher could be responsible for an error that compromised the basic evangelical doctrine of justification by faith alone. Luther and his English followers had set the whole vernacular-translation ball rolling in order that people should understand this very truth.

Biblical Inerrancy

This leads us to an issue important for conservative evangelicals: biblical inerrancy. If the canonical writings are, literally, "God-breathed", which translation from the original language actually presents us with the word of God in a form not debased by human error? In 1978 a conference of evangelical scholars meeting in Chicago produced the Chicago Statement on Biblical Inerrancy. It stated:

> *Since God has nowhere promised an inerrant*
> *transmission of Scripture, it is necessary to affirm that*
> *only the autographic text of the original documents was*
> *inspired and to maintain the need of textual criticism as*
> *a means of detecting any slips that may have crept into*
> *the text in the course of its transmission. The verdict*
> *of this science, however, is that the Hebrew and Greek*
> *text appear to be amazingly well preserved, so that we*
> *are amply justified in affirming, with the Westminster*
> *Confession, a singular providence of God in this matter*
> *and in declaring that the authority of Scripture is in no*
> *way jeopardized by the fact that the copies we possess are*
> *not entirely error-free.*
>
> *Similarly, no translation is or can be perfect, and*
> *all translations are an additional step away from the*
> *autographa. Yet the verdict of linguistic science is that*
> *English-speaking Christians, at least, are exceedingly well*
> *served in these days with a host of excellent translations*

> *and have no cause for hesitating to conclude that the true*
> *Word of God is within their reach.*[14]

For some devotees of the King James Version this cautious, considered verdict smacks of rank heresy:

> *Many Bible college students, professors, pastors, teachers*
> *and lay people talk about, "we believe in the inerrancy of*
> *the scriptures as found in the* **originals** *" – NOBODY*
> *has the originals. They are saying that we don't have*
> *God's word today which directly contradicts what Jesus*
> *said in Matthew 24:35. The faith of many young*
> *Christians is shattered by the time they leave Bible*
> *college...*
>
> *I will NEVER go to school to translate the Bible. I've*
> *got the best teacher in the universe and beyond – His name*
> *is the Holy Ghost. I've also got the word of God – the*
> *Authorized King James Bible. I have NEVER once gotten*
> *increased understanding from a preacher's "explanation of*
> *the Greek". The forceful, unabated, irreverent attack on the*
> *Authorized King James Bible that has served Christendom*
> *for almost 400 years is the result of liberalism gone*
> *amuck.*[15]

So writes one member of the American King-James-Only Movement, and the desire, or need, of some believers to have a clear, fixed, undisputed, and indisputable written text is easy to understand. Theoretically, at least, it disposes of argument. We only have to read the seventeenth-century text to grasp unambiguously what God has to say on matters of faith, morals, human relationships, politics, global concerns, and so on. Unfortunately, that position fails to dispose of the fact that Christians who share a devotion to the King James Version still manage to disagree on some issues.

And there is another more fundamental problem. One question that passionate advocates of the King James Bible have to answer is *which* version are they pinning their faith on? Is it the jumbled text which first came from Robert Barker's press in 1611? Is it the corrected text which had established itself by the time the Civil War burst on the nation? Is it Blayney's 1769 text with its 24,000 corrections to the original? One thing is clear: it is a text which has not been influenced by the *Codez Bezae*, the *Codex Alexandrinus*, the *Codex Sinaiaticus*, or any other post-1611 manuscript discoveries. Those who believe that the Authorized Version can never be improved upon are tacitly endorsing the *Textus Receptus*, which Bancroft's men relied on and which is known to contain scribal errors.

Finally, another problem the King-James-Only Movement has to cope with is the Apocrypha. This, as we have seen, was translated by the same scholars and at the same time as the books of the authorized canon. The King-James-Only devotees believe that Bancroft's team were under the special providence of God when they translated the canonical Scriptures but not when they turned their attention to the Apocrypha. They were presumably mistaken when they were inspired by God to publish both simultaneously.

The Pros and Cons of New Translations

There is, certainly, one way in which the multiplicity of translations has led to the Bible's cutting edge being dulled. Time was when verses and passages of Scripture were committed to memory as a devotional exercise or as a method of teaching the faith. The existence of one, universal translation made it easy for Christians to build up personal anthologies of texts. Remembered key verses could be used as religious currency among Christians, strengthening fellowship and reaffirming belief. The New International Version, the Good News Bible, the Jerusalem Bible, and others may be more reliable for serious study but the absence of a universal text has changed the way Christians use the Bible. The valuable *aides-memoires* no longer exist. In study groups it is now common practice for members to compare various readings in their quest for the core meaning of a given passage. This may well be helpful to them but the price paid for it has been the loss of those biblical "pegs" on which earlier generations hung their spiritual clothes.

For some people the arguments for retaining the 1611 Bible are purely cultural or nostalgic:

> *It is impossible now to experience in an English church*
> *the enveloping amalgam of tradition, intelligence, beauty,*
> *clarity of purpose, intensity of conviction and plangent,*
> *heart-gripping godliness which is the experience of page*
> *after page of the King James Bible. Nothing in our*
> *culture can match its breadth, depth and universality,*
> *unless, curiously enough, it is something that was written*
> *at exactly the same time and in almost exactly the same*
> *place: the great tragedies of Shakespeare.*[16]

So wrote Adam Nicolson in a recent book on the history of the King James Version. It is incontrovertible that this text has served the English-speaking church well for 400 years and that throughout the world there are devout men and women who continue to draw inspiration from it. For them it has become a sacred artefact whose increasingly outdated language is proof of its holiness, its origins in the realm of divine timelessness. There is obviously something to be said for having a standard, uncontested text of the Christian writings. But, as Professor Alistair McGrath of King's College London, points out, the "Englishing" of Holy Scripture,

> *will not end, until either history is brought to a close or*
> *English ceases to be a living language. The true heirs*
> *of the King James translators are those who continue*
> *their task today, not those who declare it to have been*
> *definitively concluded in 1611.*[17]

All new translators, we may charitably assume, embark on their task with conviction and enthusiasm. Do they also approach it with a sense of responsibility – one might almost say "awe" – towards biblical scholars of the past? Back in 1604 those very men charged with creating the new version experienced (or were rumoured to experience) a certain reluctance about their task.

> *It is said that both the Archbishop of Canterbury and*
> *the Bishop of London show some backwardness in this*
> *new translation of the Bible, lest the former translation*
> *done under Archbishop Parker be brought into disrepute,*
> *and hereby occasion given to the Papists of discrediting*
> *our common English Bible and the doctrines founded*
> *upon it, especially if the persons employed in the work*
> *of translating anew should affect many alterations*
> *and different readings from the former, more than be*
> *necessary.*[18]

Attempts to make the Bible more accessible run the risk of opening it to criticism from atheists and agnostics who may throw out the taunt, "Are you still not sure, after seventeen centuries or so, exactly what your sacred writings are saying?".

To translate or not to translate – that is the question. And the answer depends on our understanding of what the Bible is for – recitation or rejuvenation, celebration or cerebration, edification or emotional release. To regard the King James Bible as God's final and perfect word to the English-speaking world is to make it into an icon. Just as much as any statue, painting or stained glass image, the big, black Bible with its title page set out in Gothic lettering may become an object to be venerated for itself rather than as a conduit through which the transforming word of God flows into the human soul. C. S. Lewis pointed out the danger of the wrong kind of veneration:

> *... we must sometimes get away from the Authorised*
> *Version, if for no other reason, simply because it is so*
> *beautiful and so solemn. Beauty exalts, but beauty also*
> *lulls. Early associations endear but they also confuse.*
> *Through that beautiful solemnity the transporting or*
> *horrifying realities of which the Book tells may come to us*

blunted and disarmed and we may only sigh with tranquil
veneration when we ought to be burning with shame or
struck dumb with terror or carried out of ourselves by
ravishing hopes and adorations. Does the word "scourged"
really come home to us like "flogged"? Does "mocked
him" sting like "jeered at him"?[19]

Professor McGrath has more recently insisted, "When a translation itself requires translation, it has ceased to serve its original purpose."[20] If we are to have an English Bible at all, what we have will not be an original text delivered from heaven on plates of gold. It will be a *translation* and the chief considerations affecting its usefulness will be those of accuracy and accessibility.

The only kind of sanctity which scripture can lose by
being modernised is an accidental kind which it never had
for its writers or its earliest readers. The New Testament
in the original Greek is not a work of literary art: it is not
written in a solemn, ecclesiastical language, it is written
in the sort of Greek which was spoken over the Eastern
Mediterranean after Greek had become an international
language and therefore lost its real beauty and subtlety. In
it we see Greek used by people who have no real feeling
for Greek words because Greek words are not the words
they spoke when they were children. It is a sort of "basic"
Greek; a language without roots in the soil, a utilitarian,
commercial and administrative language... The same
divine humility which decreed that God should become a
baby at a peasant-woman's breast, and later an arrested
field-preacher in the hands of the Roman police, decreed
also that He should be preached in a vulgar, prosaic and
unliterary language. If you can stomach the one, you can
stomach the other.[21]

Anyone who values the Bible, not primarily as a work of literature but as the "lively Oracles of God", will be in no doubt that the world was never more in need of its message than it is today. To modern ears the King James Version is, if not unintelligible, at least only intelligible with great effort. As we stumble our way into the twenty-first century the translation of the Scriptures created on the instructions of the first Stuart king has, for the first time, been displaced from its position as the best-selling English Bible. Now it takes second place to the New International Version. And still scholars tread the translation trail. In 2008 The English Standard Version Study Bible made its appearance. Its publishers stand in the long tradition of those who want to (in the words of its introduction) preserve "excellence, beauty, and accuracy" while making it as easy as possible for readers "to come to a deeper understanding". Its 2,752 pages are equipped with footnotes, supplementary articles, charts, and full-colour illustrations. The makers of the Geneva Bible would certainly approve of their efforts.

Others would not. They might be tempted to agree with John Dryden that fresh translations were pearls cast before swine:

> *The Book thus put in every vulgar hand,*
> *Which each presumed he best could understand,*
> *The common rule was made the common prey*
> *And at the mercy of the rabble lay.*
> *The tender page with horny fists was galled,*
> *And he was gifted most that loudest bawled.*[22]

The open Bible is always prone to abuse and the more open it becomes (by virtue of modernization of the text), the greater the danger of individualistic and bizarre interpretation. But the remedy is not *no* fresh translation. The Bible only lives if it lives in the context of a changing world. The King James Version was made for an authoritarian age and was one of a raft of measures designed to impose unity and uniformity on the English people. Even its more fervent admirers would not want a return to that world.

The King James Version has had, and continues to have, a quite extraordinary history. It is unique in the annals of all books, published in any language, anywhere, at any time. Its influence has been and continues to be incalculable. It has helped to shape the western mind; has influenced what we think and how we think. It has changed the world. Yet, we must be careful not to lapse into idolatry for, of course, the 1611 Bible is only one vehicle carrying across the centuries and millennia a cargo of ancient wisdom, piety, and truth.

The King James Bible story is part of a bigger and more important narrative – the quest for religious certainty. Faced with the great unknowns of our existence as brief, microscopic organisms in time and space, we look for someone or something that will tell us who and why we are and what, if anything, awaits us beyond the material realm. For most Christians the answers are to be found in the word of God. But that only raises more questions – "What does this complicated library of books we call the Bible actually say?" "Who can interpret it?" "How can we understand it?" In their persistence to seek concrete answers, Christians place their faith in those who translate the ancient writings. But, surely, to lock profound mysteries in boxes padlocked with infallibility misses the point. If the Bible is a divine revelation, it is infinitely greater than the human words which convey it. It should be enough for believers to know about God what the ancient prophet knew:

> *...as the rain cometh down and the snow from heaven and*
> *... watereth the earth, and maketh it bring forth and bud,*
> *that it may give seed to the sower, and bread to the eater:*
>
> *So shall my word be that goeth forth out of my mouth: it*
> *shall not return unto me void, but it shall accomplish that*
> *which I please, and it shall prosper in the thing whereto I*
> *sent it. (Isaiah 55:10–11)*

NOTES

Chapter 1

1 *Anecdotes Historiques, etc., d'Etienne de Bourbon,* tr. and ed. A. Lecoy de la Marche for the Société de l'histoire de France, Paris, 1877, p. 365

2 J. Sumption, *Pilgrimage – an Image of Medieval Religion,* London, 1975, p. 116

3 Gregory of Tours, *In Gloria Martyrum,* XXVII, pp. 503–504

4 J. Huizinga, *The Waning of the Middle Ages,* London, 1952, p. 136

5 Quoted by R. L. P. Milburn in *The Cambridge History of the Bible,* Cambridge, 1969, II, p. 295

6 *Anecdotes Historiques, etc., d'Etienne de Bourbon,* op. cit., p. 289

Chapter 2

1 Statutes of the Realm, 2 : 12 S-28: 2 Henry IV

2 A. W. Pollard, *Records of the English Bible,* Oxford, 1911, p. 79

3 J. Wycliffe, *Summae Theologica,* VIII, p. 146

4 *The Holy Bible in the Earliest English Version Made from the Latin Vulgate by John Wycliffe and His Followers,* ed. J. Forshall and F. Madden, London, 1840

5 Cf. *Anecdotes Historiques, etc., d'Etienne de Bourbon,* op. cit., p. 307

6 J. Foxe, *Actes and Monuments,* ed. G. Townend and S. R. Cattley, London, 1841 (hereafter cited as "Foxe"), III, p. 595

7 Wycliffe's tract, *The holiprophete David seith,* reprinted in M. Deanesley, *The Lollard Bible,* London, 1920, pp. 445 ff.

8 E. Arber, *English Reprints,* London, 1926, XXVIII, p. 165

9 R. Pecock, *The Repression of Over Much Blaming of the Clergy,* ed. C. Babington, Rolls Series 19, I–II, 1860, i, pp. 53–54

10 *Christian Humanism and the Reformation. Selected Writings of Erasmus with the Life of*

Erasmus by Beatus Rhenanus, ed. J. C. Olin, New York, 1975, p. 97

11 *Erasmi Epistolae*, ed. P. S. Allen, H. M. Allen, and H. W. Garrod, London, 1906–47, III, p. 177

12 W. Tyndale, *Doctrinal Treatises and Introductions to Different Portions of the Holy Scriptures*, ed. H. Walter, Parker Society, Cambridge, 1848, p. 396

13 T. More, *Works*, ed. W. Rastell, 1557, p. 344

14 J. Strype, *Ecclesiastical Memorials*, 1816, III (2), pp. 390–91

15 H. Ellis, *Original Letters*, 1st series, London, 1824, II, p. 45

16 Quoted in C. Sturge, *Cuthbert Tunstall*, London, 1938, p. 132

17 W. Tyndale, *Doctrinal Treatises*, op. cit, p. 461

18 *The Work of William Tyndale*, ed. G. E. Duffield, London, 1964, p. 4

19 Foxe, IV, p. 676

20 This letter, the only example of Tyndale's handwriting in existence, was found among the council archives in Brabant. This translation is taken from *The Work of William Tyndale*, ed. G. E. Duffield, London, 1964, p. 401.

Chapter 3

1 R. Roper, "Life of Sir Thomas More" in R. S. Sylvester and D. P. Harding, eds., *Two Early Tudor Lives*, New Haven, 1962, p. 126

2 W. Fulke, *A Defense of the sincere and true Translations of the holie Scriptures into the English tong*, Parker Society, Cambridge, 1843, p. 98

3 W. Pollard, *Records of the English Bible*, Oxford, 1911, p. 250

4 H. Jenkyns, *The Remains of Thomas Cranmer, D.D., Archbishop of Canterbury*, London, 1833, p. 346

5 *Letters and Papers Foreign and Domestic of the Reign of Henry VIII*, ed. J. Gairdner, London, 1861–63, XIV, 897

6 Thomas Becon, *Works*, ed. J. Ayre, Parker Society, Cambridge, 1843–44, I, p.38

7 Pollard, op. cit., pp. 268–71

8 Foxe, V, p.527

9 Ibid., pp. 534–5

10 *Certayne sermons, or homilies, appointed by the Kynges Maiestie, to bee declared and redde*, etc., 1547, B. iii

11 For these and other examples, see J. F. Mozley, *Coverdale and His Bibles*, London, 1953, pp. 299 ff.

12 Preface to Whittingham's New Testament. Cf. Pollard, op.cit, p. 27739

13 Reprinted in Pollard, op. cit., p. 285

14   Ibid., pp. 297–98

15   *Letters and Memorials of Cardinal Allen*, quoted in J. G. Carleton, *The Part of Rheims in the Making of the English Bible*, London, 1902, pp. 52ff.

16   Ibid., pp. 52 ff.

Chapter 4

1   Cf. *Church and Society in England, Henry VIII to James I*, ed. F. Head and R. O'Day, London, 1977, p. 73

2   Cf. M. Aston, *England's Iconoclasts: Laws Against Images*, Oxford, 1988, p. 362

3   W. Barlow, *The Summ and Substance of the Conference which it pleased His Excellent Majesty to Have with the Lords, Bishops and Other Clergie at Hampton Court, January 14, 1603*, 1965 ed., Gainesville, Florida, p. 46

4   John Whitgift, "The Defence of the Answer to the Admonition", in *The Works of John Whitgift*, ed. J. Ayre, Parker Society, Cambridge, 1851–53, I, pp. 180 ff.

5   Ibid.

6   R. Hooker, *Laws of Ecclesiastical Polity*, VII, I, 4

7   *The Basilicon Doron of King James VI*, ed. J. Craigie, London, 1944, p. 25

8   Ibid., p. 79

9   R. Bancroft, *A Sermon Preached at St. Paul's Cross the 9 of Februarie… 1588* in W. A. Jackson, F. S. Ferguson, and K. F. Pantzer, *A Short Title Catalogue of Books 1475–1640*, 1986–91, 1346, p.87

10   W. Haller, *The Rise of Puritanism*, London, 1957, pp. 54–55

11   *Dictionary of National Biography*, Oxford, 1965 ed. (hereafter "DNB")

12   State Trials II, pp. 31–32

13   W. Barlow, op. cit., p. 45

14   State Trials II, op. cit., p. 80

15   See B. F. Westcott, *A General View of the History of the English Bible*, London, 1905 ed., pp. 112–14

16   See *The Bible in its Ancient and English Versions*, ed. H. W. Robinson, Oxford, 1940, pp. 199–200

Chapter 5

1   *Revised Standard Version*, Preface, 1952

2   W. Prynne, *Anti-Arminianisme*, 1630, Appendix

3   DNB, op. cit.

4   Cf. H. C. Porter, *Reformation and Reaction in Tudor Cambridge*, Cambridge, 1958, p. 314

5   DNB, op. cit.

6   H. R. Trevor-Roper, *Archbishop Laud, 1573–1645*, London, 1940, p. 25

7   S. R. Gardiner, *History of England from the Accession of James I to the Outbreak of the Civil War, 1603–1642*, London, 1883–84, 11 – II, p. 251

8   *Sola fidei*, meaning "by faith alone", and *sola scriptura* meaning "by scripture alone".

9   DNB, op. cit.

10 A. Wood, *Athenae Oxoniensi…*, ed. P. Bliss, London, 1813–20, II, p. 359

11 H. R. Trevor-Roper, op. cit.

12 DNB

Chapter 6

1   Cf. A. S. Cook, "The Authorised Version and its influence", in A. W. Ward and A. R. Waller, eds., *The Cambridge History of English Literature*, Cambridge, ed. A. R. Waller and A. W. Ward, 1961, IV, p. 45

2   J. B. Phillips, *Letters to Young Churches*, 1947, p. xii

3   M. H. Black, "The Printed Bible" in *Cambridge History of the Bible*, ed. S. L. Greenslade, Cambridge, 1963, II, p. 455

Chapter 7

1   W. H. Hutton, *The English Church from the Accession of Charles I to the Death of Anne (1625–1714)*, London, 1934, p. 74

2   Baedeker's *Central Italy and Rome*, 1877, p. lix

3   W. Prynne, *Histriomastix, The Player's Scourge or Actor's Tragedy*, 1633, New York, 1974, "Preface to the Christian Reader"

4   F. Bacon, *"Of Masques and Triumphs", Essays*, 1625

5   Cf. W. Heller, *The Rise of Puritanism*, New York, 1957, p. 148

6   *No Man is an Island – A selection from the prose of John Donne*, ed. R. Scott, 1997, pp. 196–97

7   *Herbert's Poems*, 1903, p. 15

8   B. Reay, "Popular Religion" in *Popular Culture in Seventeenth-Century England*, ed. B. Reay, London, 1985, pp. 94–95

9   Ibid., p. 98

10 T. Carlyle, *Oliver Cromwell's Letters and Speeches*, 1913, III, pp. 178–79

11 C. Hill, *The World Turned Upside Down: Radical Ideas during the English Revolution*, London, 1975, p. 360

12 W. Dell, "The Building, Beauty, Teaching and Establishment of the True Christian and Spiritual Church," in *Several Sermons and Discourses*, 1709, p. 109

13 Cf. C. Hill, *The English Bible and the Seventeenth Century Revolution*, London, 1994, p. 232

14 L. A. Weigle, "English Versions Since 1611" in S. L. Greenslade, op. cit., p. 364

15 Cf. A. Brockett, *Nonconformity in Exeter, 1650–1875*, Manchester, 1962, p. 46

16 Calendar of State Papers Domestic, 1674, pp. 396–97

17 *The Diary of John Evelyn*, ed. E. S. de Beer, Oxford, 1959, p. 430

18 Cf. F. E. Hutchinson, "The Sacred poets" in *The Cambridge History of English Literature*, Cambridge, 1961, VII, p. 44

Chapter 8

1 D. Mace, *The New Testament in Greek and English... corrected from the Authority of the most Authentic Manuscripts*, 1729

2 Cf. L. A. Ferell, *The Bible and the People*, New Haven, 2008, p. 121

3 Cf. S. E. Morrison, H. S. Commager, and W. E. Leuchtenburg, *A Concise History of the American Republic*, Oxford, 1983, p. 328

4 Ibid., p. 317

5 A. S. Cook, op. cit., p. 50

6 Ibid., pp. 43–46

7 Ibid., p. 50

8 G. M. Young, *Victorian England: Portrait of an Age*, London, 1936, p. 5

9 D. W. Bebbington, *Evangelicalism in Modern Britain: A History from the 1730s to the 1980s*, London, 1989, p. 149

Chapter 9

1 *Revised Version of the Bible*. Cf. also F. F. Bruce, *The English Bible*, London, 1961, p. 145

2 Cf. F. F. Bruce, op. cit., p. 150

3 Ibid., pp. 139–40

4 E. Abbot and L. Campbell, *Life and Letters of Benjamin Jowett*, 1897, I, p. 362

5 J. W. Burgon, *Inspiration and Interpretation*, 1861, p. 89

6 A. Hastings, *A History of English Christianity, 1920–85*, London, 1986, pp. 580–81

7 M. Imoukkuede, quoted by J. Donders, *Non-Bourgeois Theology*, Maryknoll, New York, 1979, p. 39

8 Cf. F. F. Bruce, op. cit., p. 161

9 J. B. Phillips, *The Gospels in Modern English*, 1950, Preface

10 *Toronto Star*, 7 April, 1996

11 *The New International Version of the Holy Bible*, 1978, Translators' Preface

Chapter 10

1 J. Barzun, *From Dawn to Decadence*, New York, 2000, p. 4

2 DNB

3 J. Donne, L. P. Smith, ed., *Donne's Sermons*, Oxford, 1920, p. 156

4 D. K. Roberts, *The Centuries' Poetry*, II, London, 1952, p. 56

5 B. Jonson, *Every Man in his Humour*, Prologue

6 A. C. Tait, *Some Thoughts on the Duties of the Established Church of England as a National Church*, London, 1876, p. 3

7 J. H. Whiteley, *Wesley's England*, London, 1938, p. 328

8 Cf. E. P. Thompson, *The Making of the English Working Class*, London, 1980, pp. 880–81

9 A. S. Cook, op. cit., IV, p. 48

10 B. Behan, *The Hostage*, 1958

11 D. Thomas, "Do Not Go Gentle into that Good Night", in *Dylan Thomas; The Poems*, ed. D. Jones, London, 1978, p. 207

12 "Articles of Religion" No. 24 in the *Book of Common Prayer*

13 J. Cascione, *A Review of the Revised "God's Word" Bible*, www.reclaimingwalther.org/articles

14 www.bible-researcher.com/chicago1.html

15 www.jesus-is-lord.com/kjvdefn2.htm

16 A. Nicolson, *Power and Glory: Jacobean England and the Making of the King James Bible*, London, 2003, p. 239

17 A. McGrath, *In the Beginning: The Story of the King James Bible*, London, 2001, p. 301

18 *A Jacobean Journal*, ed. G. B. Harrison, London, 1941, p. 108

19 C. S. Lewis in J. B. Phillips, *Letters to Young Churches*, London, 1947, Introduction, pp. viii–ix

20 A. McGrath, op. cit., p. 309

21 Ibid., p. vii

22 John Dryden, *Religio Laici*

BIBLIOGRAPHY

Abbot, E., and Campbell, L., *Life and Letters of Benjamin Jowett*, (1897), I

Abbott, W. C., ed., *The Writings and Speeches of Oliver Cromwell*, London (1937–47)

Allen, P. S., Allen H. M., and Garrod, H. W., eds., *Erasmi Epistolae*, London (1906–47), III

Allen, W., *Translating for King James: Notes Made by a Translator of King James' Bible*, Nashville, Tennessee (1969)

Anderson, C., and Prime, S. I., *Annals of the English Bible*, New York (1856)

Arber, E., *English Reprints*, XXVIII, London (1926)

Ashley, M., *Oliver Cromwell and the Puritan Revolution*, London (1958)

Aston, M., *England's Iconoclasts: Laws Against Images*, Oxford (1988)

Bacon, F. "Of Masques and Triumphs", *Essays*, 1625 ed.

Bancroft, R., *A Sermon Preached at St. Paul's Cross the 9 of Februarie…* (1588) in Jackson, W. A., Ferguson, F. S., and Pantzer, K. F., *A Short Title Catalogue of Books 1475–1640*, (1986–91)

Barker, H., *English Bible Versions: A Tercentenary Memorial of the King James Version*, New York (1911)

Barlow, W., *The Summe and Substance of the Conference which It Pleased His Excellent Majestie to Have with the Lords, Bishops, and Other of His Clergie at Hampton Court, January 14, 1603*, Costello W. T., and Kennan, C., eds., Gainsville, Florida (1965)

Barzun, J., *From Dawn to Decadence*, New York (2000)

Bebbington, D. W., *Evangelicalism in Modern Britain: A History from the 1730s to the 1980s*, London (1989)

Becon, Thomas, *Works*, ed. Ayre, J. *Parker Society*, Cambridge (1843–44), I

Black, M. H., "The Printed Bible" in *Cambridge History of the Bible*, ed. S. L. Greenslade, Cambridge (1963), II

Braidfoot, L., *The Bible and America*, Nashville, Tennesse. (1983)

Brochett, A., *Nonconformity in Exeter*, 1650–1875, Manchester (1962)

Bruce, F. F., *History of the Bible in English: From the Earliest Versions*, 3rd ed., London (1978)

Bruce, F. F., *The English Bible: A History of Translations*, London (1961)

Burgon, J. W., *Inspiration and Interpretation*, (1861)

Burnet, G., *A History of the Reformation of the Church of England*, 3 vols., Dublin (1730–32)

Caird, G., *The Language and Imagery of the Bible*, London (1980)

Carleton, J. G., *The Part of Rheims in the Making of the English Bible*, London (1902).

Carlyle, T., *Oliver Cromwell's Letters and Speeches*, 1913 ed., III

Carson, D. A., *The King James Version Debate*, Grand Rapids, Michigan (1979)

Cascione, J., *A Review of the Revised "God's Word" Bible*, www.reclaimingwalther.org/articles

Collinson, P., *The Religion of Protestants: The Church and English Society 1559–1625*, Oxford (1982)

Cook, A. S., "The Authorised Version and its influence", in A. W. Ward and A. R. Waller, eds., *The Cambridge History of English Literature*, Cambridge (1961), IV

Craigie, J., ed., *The Basilicon Doron of King James VI*, London (1944)

Cust, R., and Hughes, A., eds., *Conflict in Early Stuart England: Studies in Religion and Politics, 1607–1642*, Cambridge (1999)

Daniell, D., *William Tyndale: A Biography, New Haven*, Connecticut (1994)

Danner, D. G., "The Contribution of the Geneva Bible of 1560 to English Protestantism" in *Sixteenth Century Journal* 12 (1981)

Datches, D., *The King James Version of the English Bible. An Account of the Development and Sources of the English Bible of 1611 with Special Reference to the Hebrew Tradition*, Hamden, Connecticut (1968)

Davies, H , *Worship and Theology in England*, 5 vols., Princeton (1961 70)

Davies, J., *The Caroline Captivity of the Church: Charles I and the Remoulding of Anglicanism 1625–11*, Oxford (1992)

de Beer, E. S., ed., *The Diary of John Evelyn*, Oxford (1959)

Deanesly, M., *The Lollard Bible and Other Medieval Biblical Versions*, Cambridge (1920)

Dell, W., "The Building, Beauty, Teaching and Establishment of the True Christian and Spiritual Church", in *Several Sermons and Discourses*, 1709

Dickens, A. G., *The English Reformation*, 2nd ed., London (1989)

Donders, J., *Non-Bourgeois Theology*, Maryknoll, New York (1979)

Dryden, J., *Religio Laici*

Duffield, G. E., ed., *The Work of William Tyndale*, London (1964)

Ellis, H., *Original Letters*, 1st series, London (1824), II

Ferell, L. A., *The Bible and the People*, New Haven (2008)

Forshall, F., and Madden, F., eds., *The Holy Bible in the Earliest English Version Made from the Latin Vulgate by John Wycliffe and His Followers*, London (1840)

Frerichs, E. S., *The Bible and Bibles in America*, Atlanta, Georgia (1988)

Fry, F., *The Editions of the New Testament. Tyndale's Version 1525–1566*, London (1878)

Fulke, W., *A Defense of the sincere and true Translations of the holie Scriptures into the English tong*, Parker Society, Cambridge (1843)

Gairdner, J., ed., *Letters and Papers Foreign and Domestic of the Reign of Henry VIII*, London (1861–63), XIV

Gardiner, S. R., *History of England from the Accession of James I to the Outbreak of the Civil War, 1603–1642*, London (1883–84)

Garrett, C. H. *The Marian Exiles*, Cambridge (1938)

Geneva Bible, ed. Berry, L. E., Madison, Wisconsin (1969)

Gregg, P., *Oliver Cromwell*, London (1988)

Gregory of Tours, *In Gloria Martyrum*, XXVII

Guppy, H., and John Rylands Library, *Miles Coverdale and the English Bible, 1488–1568*, Manchester (1935)

Haller, W., *The Rise of Puritanism*, London (1957)

Hammond, G., *The Making of the English Bible*, Manchester (1982)

Harrison, G. B., ed., *A Jacobean Journal*, London (1941)

Hastings, A., *A History of English Christianity, 1920–1985*, London (1986)

Head, F., and O'Day, R., eds, *Church and Society in England, Henry VIII to James I*, London (1977)

Hill, C., *Milton and the English Revolution*, London (1977)

Hill, C., *Society and Puritanism in Pre-Revolutionary England*, London (1964)

Hill, C., *The English Bible and the Seventeenth Century Revolution*, London (1994)

Hill, C., *The World Turned Upside Down – Radical Ideas During the English Revolution*, London (1972)

Hudson, A., *The Premature Reformation: Wycliffite Texts and Lollard History*, Oxford (1988)

Huizinga, J., *The Waning of the Middle Ages*, London (1952)

Hutchinson, F. E., "The Sacred poets" in *The Cambridge History of English Literature*, Cambridge (1961), VII

Hutton, W. H., *The English Church from the Accession of Charles I to the Death of Anne (1625–1714)*, London (1934)

Jenkyns, H., *The Remains of Thomas Cranmer, D.D., Archbishop of Canterbury*, London (1833)

Lake, P., *Anglicans and Puritans? Presbyterianism and English Conformist Thought from Whitgift to Hooker*, Boston, Massachusetts (1988)

Lecoy de la Marche, A., ed., *Anecdotes Historiques, etc., d'Etienne de Bourbon*, Paris (1877)

Lewis, C. S., "The Literary Impact of the Authorised Version" in *They Asked for a Paper: Papers and Addresses*, London (1962)

MacCulloch, D., *Thomas Cranmer: A Life*, New Haven (1996)

McCullough, R. E., *Sermons at Court: Politics and Religion in Elizabethan and Jacobean Preaching*, Cambridge (1998)

McGrath, A., *In the Beginning: The Story of the King James Bible*, London (2001)

Miller, J., *Restoration England: The Reign of Charles II*, London (1985)

More, T., *Works*, ed. Rastell (1557)

Morrill, J. S., *Oliver Cromwell and the English Revolution*, London (1990)

Morrill, J. S., *The Nature of the English Revolution*, London (1993)

Morrison, S. E., Commager, H. S., and Leuchtenburg, W. E., *A Concise History of the American Republic*, Oxford (1983)

Moynaham, B., *If God Spare My Life: William Tyndale, the English Bible and Sir Thomas More*, London (2002)

Mozley, J. F., *Coverdale and His Bibles*, London (1953)

Mozley, J. F., *William Tyndale*, London (2002)

Olin, J. C., *Christian Humanism and the Reformation. Selected Writings of Erasmus with the Life of Erasmus by Beatus Rhenanus*, New York (1975)

Orlinsky, H. M., and Bratcher, R. G., *A History of Bible Translation and the North American Contribution*, Atlanta, Georgia (1991)

Parsons, G., and Moore, J. R., eds., *Religion in Victorian Britain*, 4 vols., Manchester (1988)

Pelikan, J., with Hotchkiss V. R. and Price, D., *The Reformation of the Bible/The Bible of the Reformation*, New Haven (1996)

Phillips, J. B., *Letters to Young Churches*, (1947)

Phillips, J. B., *The Gospels in Modern English*, (1950)

Pollard, A. W., *Records of the English Bible: Documents relating to the Translation and Publication of the Bible in English, 1525–1611*, Oxford (1911)

Porter, H. C., *Reformation and Reaction in Tudor Cambridge*, Cambridge (1958)

Price, A., and Ryrie, C. C., *Let It Go among Our People*, Cambridge (2004)

Prynne, W., *Anti-Arminianisme*, (1630)

Prynne, W., Histriomastix, *The Player's Scourge or Actor's Tragedy, 1633*, New York ed., (1974)

Reay, B., "Popular Religion" in Reay, B., ed., *Popular Culture in Seventeenth-Century England*, London (1985)

Robinson, H. W., ed., *The Bible in its Ancient and English Versions*, Oxford (1940)

Roper, R., "Life of Sir Thomas More" in Sylvester, R. S., and Harding, D. P., eds., *Two Early Tudor Lives*, New Haven (1962)

Ryle, J. C. ed., *Sermons and Treatises of Samuel Ward*, London (1862)

Scott, R., ed., *No Man is an Island – A selection from the prose of John Donne*, (1997)

Shriver, F., "Hampton Court Revisited: James I and the Puritans" in *Journal of Ecclesiastical History 33* (1982)

Simms, P. M., *The Bible in America: Versions that Have Played their Part in the Making of the Republic*, New York (1936)

Smith, L. P., ed., *Donne's Sermons*, Oxford (1920)

Sturge, C., *Cuthbert Tunstall*, London (1938)

Sumption, J., *Pilgrimage – an Image of Medieval Religion*, London (1975)

Tait, A. C., *Some Thoughts on the Duties of the Established Church of England as a National Church*, London (1876)

The New Testament in Greek and English… corrected from the Authority of the most Authentic Manuscripts, London (1729)

Thompson, E. P., *The Making of the English Working Class*, London (1980)

Townend, G. and Cattley, S. R., eds., *The Acts and Monuments of John Foxe*, London (1841)

Trevor-Roper, H. R., *Archbishop Laud, 1573–1645*, 3rd ed., Basingstoke (1988)

Tyacke, N., *Anti-Calvinists: The Rise of English Arminianism c.1590–1640*, Oxford (1987)

Walter, H., ed., *Doctrinal Treatises… by William Tyndale*, Parker Society, Cambridge (1848)

Westcott, B. F., *A General View of the History of the English Bible*, London 1905 ed.

White, P., *Predestination, Policy and Polemic: Conflict and Consensus in the English Church from the Reformation to the Civil War*, Cambridge (1992)

Whiteley, J. H., *Wesley's England*, London (1938)

Whitgift, J., "The Defence of the Answer to the Admonition", in *The Works of John Whitgift*, ed. Ayre, A., Parker Society, Cambridge (1851–53), I

Wood, A., *Athenae Oxoniensi…*, ed. Bliss, P., London (1813–20), II

www.bible-researcher.com/chicago

www.jesus-is-lord.com/kjvdefn2

Wycliffe, J., *Sumnae Theologica*, VIII

Young, G. M., *Victorian England: Portrait of an Age*, London (1936)

INDEX